The Official Mediterranean Diet Cookbook

Easy and Delicious Recipes for the Whole Family, **30-Day Meal Plan**, and Tips for Healthier Living. Adapted for British Tastes.

◯ **FULL COLOUR EDITION** ◯

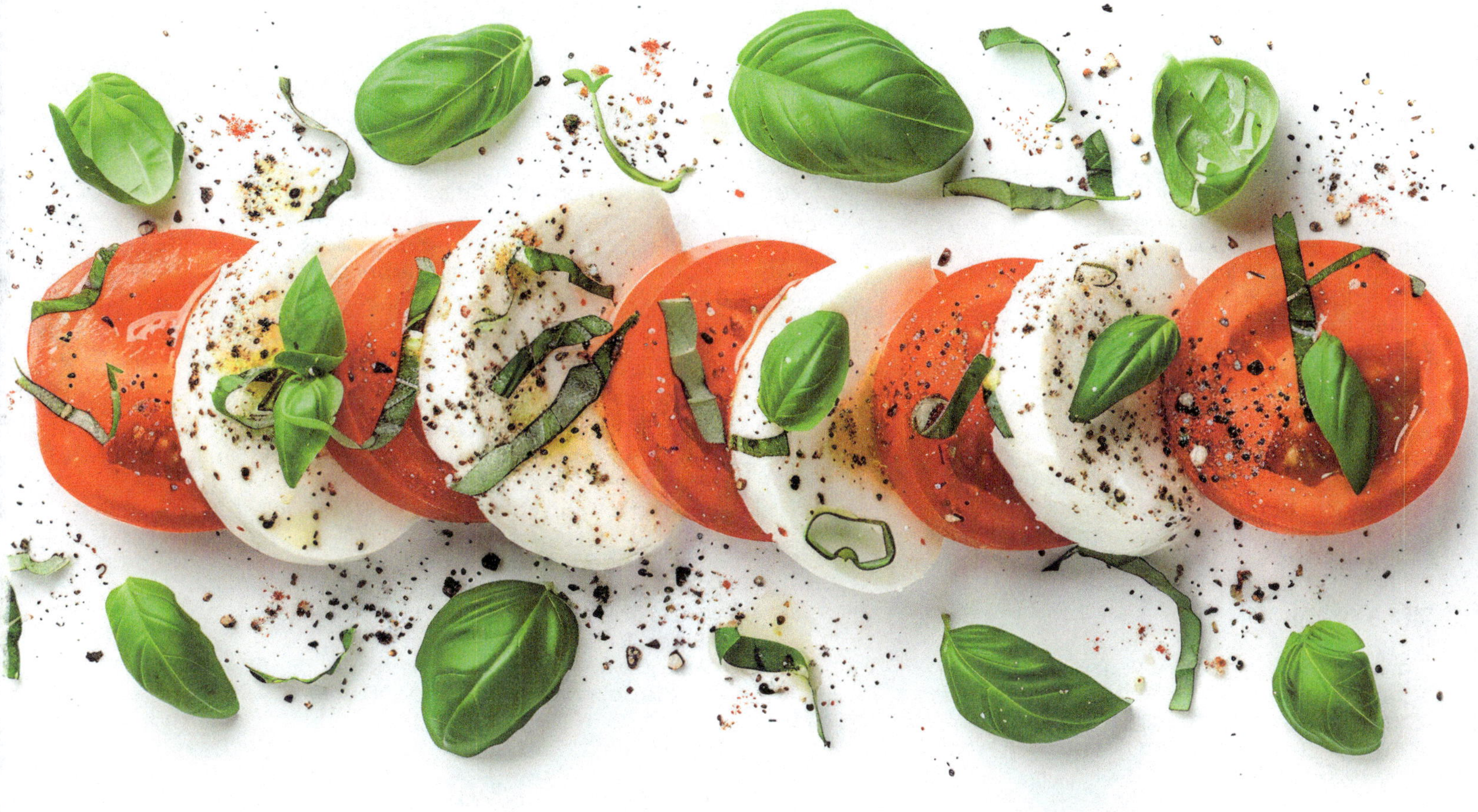

Index

1. Introduction to the Mediterranean Diet	4
2. The Core Principles of the Mediterranean Diet	6
3. Health Benefits of the Mediterranean Diet	9
4. The Mediterranean Diet in the UK Context	12
5. Guide to the 30-Day Meal Plan	15
6. The Philosophy of "Eating Well"	19
7. Tools and Accessories for Mediterranean Cooking	22
8. FAQ About the Mediterranean Diet	25
9. Conclusion of the Theoretical Section	29

BREAKFAST — 32

Greek Yogurt with Honey and Walnuts	33
Mediterranean Scrambled Eggs with Spinach and Feta	33
Avocado Toast with Cherry Tomatoes and Olive Oil	34
Overnight Oats with Almonds and Berries	34
Tomato and Cucumber Breakfast Salad	35
Whole Grain Porridge with Fresh Fruits and Nuts	35
Olive Oil and Orange Cake Muffins	36
Mediterranean Wrap with Eggs, Spinach, and Feta	36
Savory Greek Yogurt Bowl with Olives and Cucumbers	37
Ricotta and Honey on Whole Grain Toast	37
Herbed Frittata with Courgettes and Parmesan	38
Chia Pudding with Almond Milk and Fresh Fruit	38
Spinach and Mushroom Breakfast Quesadilla	39
Lemon and Poppy Seed Breakfast Loaf	39
Fig and Walnut Breakfast Bars	40
Grilled Halloumi and Tomato Sandwich	40
Mediterranean Breakfast Bowl with Quinoa and Hummus	41
Smoked Salmon and Avocado on Rye Bread	41
Egg and Vegetable Breakfast Muffins	42
Ricotta Pancakes with Berries	42

SOUP AND SALADS — 43

Greek Lentil Soup (Fakes)	44
Minestrone Soup with Seasonal Vegetables	44
Tomato and Basil Soup with Olive Oil	45
Roasted Red Pepper and Tomato Soup	45
Chickpea and Spinach Soup	46
Greek Salad with Feta and Olives	46
Quinoa Salad with Cucumber and Mint	47
Lentil and Beetroot Salad with Feta	47
Grilled Vegetable Salad with Balsamic Glaze	48
Orzo Salad with Sun-Dried Tomatoes	48
Chilled Cucumber and Yogurt Soup (Tzatziki Soup)	49
Warm Farro and Roasted Vegetable Salad	49
Cauliflower and Broccoli Soup	50
Greek Chickpea Salad with Lemon Vinaigrette	50
Tuscan White Bean and Kale Soup	51
Tabbouleh with Fresh Parsley and Mint	51
Roasted Butternut Squash and Lentil Salad	52
Spicy Carrot and Coriander Soup	52
Watermelon and Feta Salad with Fresh Mint	53
Caprese Salad with Fresh Basil and Balsamic Reduction	53

DIPS AND SAUCES — 54

Classic Hummus with Extra Virgin Olive Oil	55
Baba Ganoush (Roasted Aubergine Dip)	55
Tzatziki (Cucumber and Yogurt Dip)	56
Muhammara (Roasted Red Pepper and Walnut Dip)	56
Roasted Garlic and Lemon Aioli	57
Spicy Harissa Sauce	57
Olive Tapenade with Capers and Anchovies	58
Greek Skordalia (Garlic and Potato Dip)	58
Sun-Dried Tomato Pesto	59
Herbed Yogurt Sauce with Dill and Mint	59
Roasted Red Pepper and Feta Dip	60
Lemon and Herb Tahini Sauce	60
Avocado and Cilantro Dip	61
Green Olive and Almond Tapenade	61
Smoked Paprika Aioli	62
Fresh Tomato and Basil Salsa	62
Garlic and Lemon Tahini Dressing	63
Chimichurri Sauce with Parsley and Oregano	63
Pesto Genovese with Basil and Pine Nuts	64
Lemon-Caper Vinaigrette	64

VEGETABLES — 65

Roasted Mediterranean Vegetables with Thyme	66
Stuffed Peppers with Quinoa and Feta	66
Sautéed Spinach with Garlic and Pine Nuts	67
Ratatouille with Fresh Herbs	67
Grilled Aubergine with Tahini and Pomegranate	68
Roasted Cauliflower with Cumin and Coriander	68
Baked Tomatoes Stuffed with Rice and Herbs	69
Courgette Fritters with Tzatziki	69
Braised Green Beans with Tomatoes and Onions	70
Crispy Oven-Roasted Potatoes with Rosemary	70
Sautéed Mushrooms with Garlic and Parsley	71
Caramelised Onions and Peppers	71
Grilled Asparagus with Lemon and Olive Oil	72
Marinated Artichoke Hearts	72
Spinach and Ricotta Stuffed Aubergines	73
Herbed Roasted Carrots	73
Greek-Style Roasted Potatoes with Lemon and Oregano	74
Balsamic Glazed Brussels Sprouts	74
Roasted Butternut Squash with Sage	75
Sweet Potato Wedges with Smoked Paprika	75

SEAFOOD — 76

Grilled Salmon with Lemon and Dill	77
Garlic Prawns with Olive Oil and Parsley	77
Baked Cod with Tomatoes and Olives	78
Pan-Seared Sea Bass with Caper Sauce	78
Mussels in White Wine and Garlic	79
Tuna Salad with Olives and Red Onions	79
Grilled Sardines with Lemon and Herbs	80
Mediterranean Fish Stew with Saffron	80
Baked Trout with Almonds and Herbs	81
Grilled Calamari with Lemon and Garlic	81
Spaghetti with Clams (Spaghetti alle Vongole)	82
Prawn and Avocado Salad	82
Mediterranean Baked Fish with Vegetables	83
Smoked Mackerel Pâté	83
Shrimp and Tomato Skewers	84
Seafood Paella with Saffron	84
Oven-Baked Scallops with Lemon and Garlic	85
Grilled Tuna Steak with Fresh Herbs	85
Anchovy and Garlic Bruschetta	86
Baked Salmon with a Mustard-Dill Glaze	86

MEAT — 87

Grilled Chicken Souvlaki with Tzatziki	88

Lamb Kofta with Mint Yogurt	88
Baked Chicken Thighs with Olives and Lemon	89
Beef and Vegetable Kebabs	89
Slow-Cooked Lamb Shoulder with Rosemary	90
Mediterranean Chicken Stew with Tomatoes and Olives	90
Pork Tenderloin with Garlic and Thyme	91
Stuffed Chicken Breast with Spinach and Feta	91
Greek Meatballs (Keftedes) with Tomato Sauce	92
Roast Leg of Lamb with Garlic and Herbs	92
Grilled Pork Chops with Rosemary and Lemon	93
Chicken Tagine with Apricots and Almonds	93
Beef Moussaka with Aubergines	94
Braised Beef with Red Wine and Rosemary	94
Chicken Cacciatore with Mushrooms and Peppers	95
Spicy Lamb Meatballs with Harissa	95
Roast Chicken with Mediterranean Vegetables	96
Beef and Tomato Stew with Cinnamon	96
Marinated Grilled Lamb Chops	97
Stuffed Peppers with Ground Beef and Rice	97

DESSERTS 98

Greek Yogurt with Honey and Walnuts	99
Olive Oil and Almond Cake	99
Lemon Sorbet with Fresh Mint	100
Baklava with Pistachios and Honey	100
Almond and Orange Cake	101
Greek Rice Pudding (Rizogalo)	101
Fresh Fruit Salad with Lemon and Honey	102
Fig and Walnut Bars	102
Ricotta Cheesecake with Lemon Zest	103
Apricot and Almond Tart	103
Lemon and Yogurt Cake	104
Panna Cotta with Berry Compote	104
Roasted Pears with Honey and Cinnamon	105
Greek Almond Cookies (Amygdalota)	105
Lemon Drizzle Cake	106
Chocolate and Olive Oil Mousse	106
Spiced Orange and Almond Muffins	107
Honey and Sesame Seed Bars (Pasteli)	107
Mediterranean Fruit Compote	108
Baked Apples with Cinnamon and Nuts	108

MEAL PLAN 109

SHOPPING LIST 113

dietary habits of people in the United States, Japan, and several European countries, including Greece and Italy. The findings highlighted the health benefits of the Mediterranean diet, particularly in reducing the risk of heart disease, and laid the groundwork for its global recognition.

A BRIEF HISTORY AND ORIGINS OF THE MEDITERRANEAN DIET

The Mediterranean diet has its roots deeply embedded in the culinary traditions and lifestyle practices of the countries surrounding the Mediterranean Sea. This region, often referred to as the "Mediterranean basin," encompasses southern European countries like Italy, Greece, Spain, and parts of France, as well as North African and Middle Eastern nations such as Morocco, Turkey, and Lebanon. These diverse cultures share a common approach to food, one that has been shaped over centuries by geography, climate, and agricultural practices.

The origins of the Mediterranean diet can be traced back to ancient civilizations such as the Greeks, Romans, and Egyptians. These societies developed diets that were heavily influenced by the abundant availability of olive oil, fruits, vegetables, whole grains, and seafood in their regions. The diet was not just about sustenance but was also deeply connected to the social and cultural practices of these communities. Meals were seen as a time to gather with family and friends, and this emphasis on community and shared meals is still a cornerstone of the Mediterranean lifestyle today.

One of the most significant historical references to the Mediterranean diet comes from the island of Crete, where researchers in the mid-20th century observed remarkably low rates of chronic diseases and high life expectancy among its population. This observation was part of the landmark Seven Countries Study led by American scientist Ancel Keys, which began in the 1950s. The study investigated the

WHY THE MEDITERRANEAN DIET IS CONSIDERED ONE OF THE HEALTHIEST DIETS IN THE WORLD

The Mediterranean diet has gained widespread acclaim as one of the healthiest dietary patterns in the world. Its reputation is not based on a single study or a fleeting trend but on decades of research that consistently demonstrates its numerous health benefits.

At the core of the Mediterranean diet is its emphasis on whole, minimally processed foods. Fresh fruits and vegetables, whole grains, legumes, nuts, and seeds form the foundation of daily meals. These foods are rich in essential nutrients, including vitamins, minerals, fiber, and antioxidants, which contribute to overall health and well-being. The diet also includes healthy fats, particularly from olive oil, which is a key component of the Mediterranean diet. Olive oil is high in monounsaturated fats, which have been shown to reduce levels of "bad" LDL cholesterol and increase "good" HDL cholesterol, thereby promoting heart health.

Another reason the Mediterranean diet is highly regarded is its moderate approach to protein intake, with a focus on fish and seafood as primary sources. These are rich in omega-3 fatty acids, which are known to have anti-inflammatory properties and play a crucial role in brain health. Poultry and dairy are consumed in moderate amounts, while red meat and processed foods are limited, aligning with recommendations for reducing the risk of chronic diseases.

The Mediterranean diet is not just about what to eat but also about how to eat. It encourages mindful eating and the enjoyment of food as part of a balanced lifestyle. Meals are often shared with family and friends, fostering a sense of community and connection, which has been linked to improved mental and emotional well-being.

Numerous studies have shown that the Mediterranean diet can help prevent a variety of health conditions, including heart disease, stroke, type 2 diabetes, and certain types of cancer. It has also been associated with better weight management, improved cognitive function, and increased longevity. The diet's emphasis on plant-based foods, healthy fats, and lean protein, combined with regular physical activity and a focus on social connections, contributes to its holistic approach to health.

ADAPTING THE MEDITERRANEAN DIET FOR THE UK MARKET

While the Mediterranean diet is rooted in the specific cultural and agricultural context of the Mediterranean region, it can be effectively adapted to fit the lifestyle and food availability in the UK. The key to successfully adopting the Mediterranean diet in the UK lies in maintaining its core principles while making practical adjustments that align with local tastes and ingredient availability.

One of the most significant adaptations involves sourcing ingredients. In the Mediterranean, fresh, locally-grown produce is readily available, and this is a hallmark of the diet. In the UK, while some Mediterranean staples like olive oil, tomatoes, and certain fruits and vegetables are accessible year-round, others may be seasonal or less common. However, UK consumers can still embrace the diet by focusing on locally-sourced produce when possible, opting for seasonal vegetables and fruits, and utilizing farmers' markets and organic food suppliers.

Another adaptation involves incorporating UK culinary traditions into the Mediterranean framework. For example, instead of solely relying on Mediterranean herbs and spices, UK residents can use familiar flavors like fresh mint, thyme, or parsley, which are widely available and can be grown in local gardens. Traditional British dishes can also be given a Mediterranean twist by using olive oil instead of butter or incorporating more vegetables and legumes into recipes.

The UK also offers a variety of fish and seafood that can be seamlessly integrated into the Mediterranean diet. While fish like sardines and anchovies are staples in Mediterranean countries, UK residents can substitute these with locally-sourced options like mackerel, herring, or trout, which are equally rich in omega-3 fatty acids and offer similar health benefits.

Furthermore, adapting the Mediterranean diet to the UK market involves addressing the eating habits and lifestyle of the British population. The Mediterranean diet promotes leisurely, communal meals, which may differ from the faster-paced, often solitary dining experiences common in the UK. Encouraging a shift towards more mindful eating practices, such as taking time to savor meals and incorporating more family meals into the week, can enhance the overall effectiveness of the diet.

Lastly, the Mediterranean diet can be adapted to fit into the UK's colder climate, where hearty, warming dishes are often preferred. This can be achieved by incorporating more soups, stews, and roasted vegetable dishes, all of which align with the Mediterranean approach to cooking and can be made with ingredients available in the UK.

In summary, the Mediterranean diet's adaptability is one of its strengths, allowing individuals in the UK to enjoy its health benefits while incorporating local flavors and ingredients. By focusing on fresh, whole foods, healthy fats, and a balanced approach to meals, UK residents can successfully adopt this time-honored dietary pattern and integrate it into their daily lives.

KEY COMPONENTS: FRUITS, VEGETABLES, LEGUMES, WHOLE GRAINS, FISH, OLIVE OIL, AND NUTS

The Mediterranean diet is celebrated for its emphasis on whole, natural foods that provide essential nutrients while supporting overall health. The foundation of this dietary pattern is built on a rich variety of plant-based foods and healthy fats, combined with moderate amounts of protein, particularly from fish and seafood. Understanding these key components is crucial to adopting the Mediterranean diet in a way that maximises its health benefits.

1. **Fruits and Vegetables:**
- Fruits and vegetables are at the heart of the Mediterranean diet. They are consumed in large quantities, often making up the majority of a meal. These foods are packed with vitamins, minerals, and antioxidants, which play a vital role in protecting the body from chronic diseases such as heart disease and cancer.
- A typical Mediterranean meal will feature a wide array of colourful vegetables, such as tomatoes, peppers, aubergines, courgettes, and leafy greens like spinach and kale. These are often grilled, roasted, or enjoyed raw in salads. Fruits, particularly citrus fruits, grapes, and berries, are frequently eaten as snacks or desserts, offering a natural source of sweetness without the need for added sugars.

2. **Legumes:**
- Legumes such as beans, lentils, and chickpeas are another cornerstone of the Mediterranean diet. They are an excellent source of plant-based protein, fibre, and essential nutrients like iron and magnesium. Legumes are incredibly versatile and can be used in a variety of dishes, from soups and stews to salads and dips like hummus.
- In the Mediterranean region, legumes are often combined with grains or vegetables to create satisfying, nutrient-dense meals. They are also valued for their ability to provide long-lasting energy and promote a feeling of fullness, making them an ideal component of a balanced diet.

3. **Whole Grains:**
- Whole grains such as whole wheat, barley, oats, and brown rice are preferred over refined grains in the Mediterranean diet. These grains are rich in dietary fibre, which supports digestive health and helps maintain steady blood sugar levels. Whole grains also provide essential vitamins and minerals, including B vitamins and iron.
- Bread, particularly whole grain or sourdough varieties, is a staple in many Mediterranean meals. However, unlike in many Western diets, bread is typically eaten in moderation and often as an accompaniment to vegetables, olive oil, and lean proteins, rather than as the main component of a meal.

4. **Fish and Seafood:**
- Fish and seafood are primary sources of protein in the Mediterranean diet, consumed several times a week. Fatty fish like salmon, mackerel, sardines, and anchovies are especially prized for their high content of omega-3 fatty acids, which have been shown to reduce inflammation, lower the risk of heart disease, and support brain health.
- In addition to omega-3s, fish provides important nutrients such as vitamin D, iodine, and selenium. Seafood is often grilled, baked, or stewed, and is commonly paired with vegetables, whole grains, and olive oil to create balanced, flavourful dishes.

5. **Olive Oil:**
- Olive oil is perhaps the most iconic component of the Mediterranean diet. It is the primary source of fat and is used generously in cooking, dressing salads, and drizzling over finished dishes. Extra virgin olive oil, in

particular, is rich in monounsaturated fats, which have been linked to improved heart health and reduced levels of LDL cholesterol.
- Beyond its healthy fat content, olive oil is also packed with antioxidants, including polyphenols, which have anti-inflammatory properties and may protect against chronic diseases. The use of olive oil in place of saturated fats like butter is a key factor in the health benefits associated with the Mediterranean diet.

6. **Nuts and Seeds:**
- Nuts and seeds are commonly consumed as snacks or added to dishes for extra flavour and texture. Almonds, walnuts, and sunflower seeds are particularly popular. They are rich in healthy fats, protein, fibre, and a variety of vitamins and minerals, including vitamin E and magnesium.
- Nuts and seeds contribute to heart health by helping to lower cholesterol levels and reduce inflammation. However, they are energy-dense, so they are typically consumed in moderation, often as part of a meal or as a light snack.

THE ROLE OF PROTEIN: FISH, LEAN MEAT, LEGUMES, AND DAIRY

Protein is an essential macronutrient that plays a critical role in building and repairing tissues, supporting immune function, and maintaining muscle mass. The Mediterranean diet includes a variety of protein sources, each offering unique benefits and contributing to the overall balance of the diet.

1. **Fish and Seafood:**
- As mentioned earlier, fish and seafood are the preferred sources of protein in the Mediterranean diet. They are consumed several times a week, often in place of red meat. The focus on fish, particularly fatty varieties, ensures a regular intake of omega-3 fatty acids, which are crucial for cardiovascular health.
- In Mediterranean cuisine, fish is typically prepared in a way that preserves its nutritional value, such as grilling, baking, or steaming. It is often served with vegetables, whole grains, and a drizzle of olive oil, making for a meal that is both satisfying and health-promoting.

2. **Lean Meat:**
- While fish and seafood are central to the Mediterranean diet, lean meats such as chicken and turkey are also consumed, albeit in smaller quantities. Red meat, such as beef and lamb, is eaten only occasionally, often reserved for special occasions or as a minor ingredient in a dish.
- When meat is included in the diet, it is typically prepared simply, often grilled or roasted, and served with plenty of vegetables and whole grains. The Mediterranean approach to meat is one of moderation, recognising it as a source of high-quality protein but not a daily necessity.

3. **Legumes:**
- Legumes, including beans, lentils, and chickpeas, are a key plant-based source of protein in the Mediterranean diet. They are often used as the main protein component of a meal, providing a hearty, filling alternative to meat.
- In addition to their protein content, legumes are rich in fibre and other nutrients that support digestive health and contribute to a feeling of fullness. Their versatility in the kitchen means they can be used in everything from soups and stews to salads and side dishes.

4. **Dairy:**
- Dairy products are included in the Mediterranean diet, but they are typically consumed in moderation. Cheese and yogurt are the most common forms of dairy, often enjoyed in small amounts as part of a meal.
- Mediterranean cheeses, such as feta, Parmesan, and pecorino, are usually used to add flavour to dishes rather than being consumed in large quantities. Yogurt, particularly Greek yogurt, is valued for its probiotic content, which supports gut health. It is often eaten with fruits and nuts as part of breakfast or a light snack.

MODERATION AND LIFESTYLE: THE IMPORTANCE OF PORTIONS AND CONVIVIALITY

The Mediterranean diet is not just about what you eat, but also how you eat. Moderation and conviviality are two core principles that underpin the Mediterranean approach to food and nutrition, ensuring that meals are both healthful and enjoyable.

1. **Moderation:**
- Moderation is a key concept in the Mediterranean diet, particularly when it comes to portion sizes and the consumption of certain foods like meat, sweets, and alcohol. The diet emphasises eating until you are satisfied, not stuffed, and encourages mindful eating practices that help individuals listen to their bodies' hunger and fullness cues.
- Portion control is naturally integrated into Mediterranean meals through the use of smaller plates, the inclusion of a variety of dishes that encourage sharing, and the emphasis on plant-based foods that are low in calories but high in nutrients. This approach helps prevent overeating and supports weight management.

2. **Conviviality:**
- Conviviality, or the enjoyment of shared meals, is a fundamental aspect of the Mediterranean lifestyle. Meals are seen as a time to gather with family and friends, to slow down, and to savour not just the food, but the experience of eating together.
- This social aspect of eating promotes mental and emotional well-being, as it strengthens relationships and provides a sense of community and belonging. In Mediterranean cultures, meals are often leisurely affairs, with multiple courses and plenty of time to enjoy conversation and company.
- The act of eating together also encourages healthier food choices, as meals prepared and consumed at home tend to be more nutritious and balanced than those eaten on the go or at restaurants. Additionally, the practice of sharing food promotes portion control, as dishes are often served family-style, allowing individuals to take only what they need.

In summary, the core principles of the Mediterranean diet—focusing on whole, natural foods; incorporating a variety of protein sources; and embracing moderation and conviviality—create a dietary pattern that is both nourishing and sustainable. By adopting these principles, individuals can enjoy a way of eating that not only supports physical health but also enhances the pleasure and social aspects of food.

3. Health Benefits of the Mediterranean Diet

The Mediterranean diet is not just a way of eating; it is a comprehensive approach to health and well-being that has been extensively studied and endorsed by medical professionals worldwide. This dietary pattern is associated with a wide range of health benefits, making it one of the most effective diets for promoting long-term health and preventing chronic diseases. Below, we explore the specific health benefits of the Mediterranean diet, including its positive effects on cardiovascular health, weight management, blood sugar control, chronic disease prevention, and cognitive function.

CARDIOVASCULAR BENEFITS: HOW THE DIET CAN IMPROVE HEART HEALTH

One of the most well-documented benefits of the Mediterranean diet is its ability to promote cardiovascular health. Numerous studies have shown that following this diet can significantly reduce the risk of heart disease, which remains the leading cause of death in many parts of the world, including the UK.

1. **Healthy Fats:**
- The Mediterranean diet is rich in healthy fats, particularly monounsaturated fats from olive oil and polyunsaturated fats from fish and nuts. These fats play a crucial role in maintaining heart health by reducing levels of low-density lipoprotein (LDL) cholesterol, often referred to as "bad" cholesterol, which can accumulate in the arteries and lead to atherosclerosis—a condition where the arteries harden and narrow, increasing the risk of heart attacks and strokes.
- Additionally, the omega-3 fatty acids found in fatty fish like salmon, mackerel, and sardines have anti-inflammatory properties and help to lower blood pressure, reduce triglycerides, and prevent the formation of blood clots. These effects collectively contribute to a healthier cardiovascular system.

2. **Antioxidants and Fibre:**
- The Mediterranean diet is also abundant in fruits, vegetables, whole grains, and legumes, all of which are excellent sources of dietary fibre and antioxidants. Fibre helps to lower cholesterol levels by binding to cholesterol in the digestive system and facilitating its removal from the body. This reduces the overall amount of cholesterol that enters the bloodstream.
- Antioxidants, including vitamins C and E, flavonoids, and polyphenols found in fruits, vegetables, and olive oil, help to protect the cardiovascular system by neutralising free radicals—unstable molecules that can cause oxidative stress and damage to cells. This antioxidant protection helps to prevent the development of atherosclerosis and other heart-related conditions.

3. **Moderation of Red Meat and Processed Foods:**
- The Mediterranean diet encourages limited consumption of red meat and processed foods, which are high in saturated fats and sodium—both of which can negatively impact heart health. By focusing on lean proteins, such as fish and poultry, and by incorporating plenty of plant-based meals, the diet helps to keep blood pressure and cholesterol levels within a healthy range.

4. **Impact on Blood Pressure:**
- High blood pressure, or hypertension, is a major risk factor for heart disease and stroke. The Mediterranean diet's emphasis on fresh, whole foods and its reduction of salt intake (through limiting processed foods) contribute to better blood pressure management. Potassium-rich foods like fruits and vegetables further support healthy blood pressure levels by balancing the effects of sodium in the body.

WEIGHT MANAGEMENT AND BLOOD SUGAR CONTROL

Another significant benefit of the Mediterranean diet is its effectiveness in supporting weight management and maintaining healthy blood sugar levels. These factors are crucial in preventing obesity, type 2 diabetes, and metabolic syndrome.

1. **Balanced and Satiating Meals:**
- The Mediterranean diet naturally supports weight management by promoting meals that are balanced in macronutrients—carbohydrates, proteins, and fats. The inclusion of high-fibre foods like vegetables, legumes, and whole grains helps to increase satiety, meaning that individuals feel fuller for longer after eating. This can reduce overall calorie intake and prevent overeating.
- Moreover, the diet's focus on healthy fats, such as those found in olive oil, nuts, and avocados, provides a satisfying texture and flavour to meals, further enhancing satiety and reducing the likelihood of snacking on less healthy options.

2. **Low Glycaemic Index Foods:**
- Many of the carbohydrates included in the Mediterranean diet, such as whole grains, fruits, and legumes, have a low glycaemic index (GI). This means they are digested and absorbed more slowly, leading to a gradual rise in blood sugar levels rather than sharp spikes. This slow and steady release of glucose into the bloodstream helps to maintain stable energy levels and reduces the risk of insulin resistance—a key factor in the development of type 2 diabetes.
- Additionally, the consumption of fibre-rich foods in the diet helps to slow the absorption of sugars, further stabilising blood sugar levels and improving insulin sensitivity.

3. **Weight Loss and Obesity Prevention:**
- Studies have shown that the Mediterranean diet can be effective for weight loss and for preventing weight gain over time. Its emphasis on whole, nutrient-dense foods means that individuals can consume fewer calories while still meeting their nutritional needs. The diet also discourages the consumption of calorie-dense, nutrient-poor processed foods that contribute to weight gain.
- Regular physical activity, which is a key component of the Mediterranean lifestyle, also plays a role in weight management. The diet encourages a holistic approach to health that includes not just dietary changes but also an active lifestyle, further supporting weight loss and the maintenance of a healthy weight.

REDUCING THE RISK OF CHRONIC DISEASES (DIABETES, HYPERTENSION, ETC.)

The Mediterranean diet's ability to reduce the risk of chronic diseases is one of the reasons it has been widely recommended by health professionals. Its nutrient-rich, anti-inflammatory properties make it a powerful tool for preventing conditions such as type 2 diabetes, hypertension, and certain cancers.

1. **Diabetes Prevention:**
- The Mediterranean diet's low glycaemic load, combined with its emphasis on whole grains, legumes, fruits, and vegetables, makes it particularly effective in reducing the risk of type 2 diabetes. By promoting stable blood sugar levels and improving insulin sensitivity, the diet helps to prevent the onset of this chronic condition.
- Furthermore, the inclusion of healthy fats, particularly from olive oil and nuts, has been shown to improve glucose metabolism, further reducing the risk of diabetes.

2. **Hypertension:**
- As mentioned earlier, the Mediterranean diet is effective in managing and preventing hypertension due to its emphasis on fresh, whole foods and its low intake of sodium. The diet's high content of potassium-rich foods, such as fruits and vegetables, also helps to regulate blood pressure by counteracting the effects of sodium.
- By maintaining healthy blood pressure levels, the Mediterranean diet reduces the risk of complications such as heart disease, stroke, and kidney damage.

3. **Cancer Prevention:**
- The Mediterranean diet's high intake of antioxidants, fibre, and healthy fats has been linked to a reduced risk of certain cancers, particularly those of the digestive tract, such as colorectal cancer. The diet's emphasis on plant-based foods provides a rich source of phytochemicals, which are natural compounds that have been shown to protect cells from DNA damage and inhibit the growth of cancer cells.
- Additionally, the diet's low consumption of red and processed meats, which have been associated with an increased risk of colorectal cancer, further contributes to its protective effects against cancer.

4. **Other Chronic Conditions:**
- The anti-inflammatory properties of the Mediterranean diet, derived from its high content of fruits, vegetables, whole grains, and healthy fats, also play a role in reducing the risk of other chronic conditions, such as rheumatoid arthritis and neurodegenerative diseases like Alzheimer's. By reducing inflammation throughout the body, the diet helps to protect against the development and progression of these diseases.

COGNITIVE BENEFITS AND MENTAL WELL-BEING

Beyond its physical health benefits, the Mediterranean diet also has a positive impact on cognitive function and mental well-being. The diet's nutrient-rich composition supports brain health and may reduce the risk of cognitive decline and mental health disorders.

1. **Cognitive Function:**
- Several studies have suggested that the Mediterranean diet is associated with better cognitive function and a lower risk of cognitive decline in older adults. The diet's high content of antioxidants, omega-3 fatty acids, and polyphenols from fruits, vegetables, olive oil, and fish supports brain health by reducing oxidative stress and inflammation—both of which are linked to cognitive decline and neurodegenerative diseases like Alzheimer's.
- The diet also supports the maintenance of healthy blood vessels, which is crucial for ensuring adequate blood flow to the brain. This, in turn, helps to preserve cognitive function as individuals age.

2. **Mental Health:**
- Emerging research indicates that the Mediterranean diet may also have a protective effect against mental health disorders, such as depression and anxiety. The diet's anti-inflammatory properties, combined with its ability to promote stable blood sugar levels and provide essential nutrients like omega-3 fatty acids, B vitamins, and magnesium, support overall mental well-being.
- The Mediterranean lifestyle, which emphasises social connections and the enjoyment of meals with others, also contributes to better mental health by reducing feelings of loneliness and social isolation—factors that are strongly associated with depression.

3. **Reduced Risk of Dementia:**
- There is growing evidence to suggest that adherence to the Mediterranean diet may reduce the risk of developing dementia, including Alzheimer's disease. The diet's emphasis on healthy fats, particularly omega-3s, along with its high content of antioxidant-rich foods, helps to protect brain cells from damage and supports the maintenance of cognitive function in later life.

In conclusion, the Mediterranean diet offers a wide array of health benefits, from improving heart health and managing weight to reducing the risk of chronic diseases and supporting cognitive function. Its holistic approach to nutrition and lifestyle makes it a powerful tool for promoting long-term health and well-being. By adopting the Mediterranean diet, individuals can enjoy a way of eating that is not only delicious and satisfying but also profoundly beneficial for their overall health.

4. The Mediterranean Diet in the UK Context

The Mediterranean diet is renowned for its emphasis on fresh, seasonal ingredients, many of which are native to the countries bordering the Mediterranean Sea. However, adopting this diet in the UK requires some adjustments due to differences in climate, agriculture, and food availability. Fortunately, with a few thoughtful adaptations, it is entirely possible to enjoy the benefits of the Mediterranean diet while making the most of what is available in British supermarkets and local markets.

ADAPTING MEDITERRANEAN INGREDIENTS TO THOSE AVAILABLE IN THE UK

The Mediterranean diet traditionally includes a variety of fruits, vegetables, legumes, whole grains, fish, and healthy fats like olive oil. While many of these ingredients are readily available in the UK, some Mediterranean staples might be less common or more expensive due to import costs. The key to successfully adapting the Mediterranean diet in the UK lies in selecting local and seasonal alternatives that offer similar nutritional benefits and flavours.

1. Fruits and Vegetables:

In the Mediterranean region, fresh produce is abundant year-round due to the warm climate. In the UK, however, the growing season is shorter, and some fruits and vegetables may not be available or as flavourful out of season. To adapt, focus on purchasing seasonal British produce whenever possible. For example:

- Tomatoes: While Mediterranean tomatoes are known for their rich flavour, British-grown tomatoes can be equally delicious when in season. In the colder months, consider using canned tomatoes or passata, which are often made from ripe, sun-drenched tomatoes, to maintain the depth of flavour in your dishes.
- Leafy Greens: In place of Mediterranean greens like chard or wild greens, opt for British-grown kale, spinach, or cabbage. These vegetables are widely available and can be used in similar ways, whether sautéed, steamed, or added to soups and stews.
- Root Vegetables: While Mediterranean diets often feature vegetables like aubergines and courgettes, root vegetables such as carrots, parsnips, and beetroots are more commonly grown in the UK. These can be roasted, mashed, or added to stews to create hearty, flavourful dishes that align with the principles of the Mediterranean diet.

2. Legumes and Grains:

- Legumes such as chickpeas, lentils, and beans are central to the Mediterranean diet and are fortunately easy to find in the UK. British supermarkets typically stock a wide variety of dried and canned legumes, making it convenient to incorporate these nutrient-dense foods into your meals.
- When it comes to grains, while whole wheat and barley are staples in both Mediterranean and British diets, you might find that oats and spelt are more readily available and locally grown in the UK. These grains can be used in place of traditional Mediterranean grains to create satisfying, fibre-rich dishes.

3. Fish and Seafood:

Fish is a cornerstone of the Mediterranean diet, particularly oily fish like sardines, mackerel, and anchovies, which are rich in omega-3 fatty acids. In the UK, you can find an excellent variety of locally caught fish that offer similar health benefits:

- Mackerel: A sustainable and affordable option, mackerel is abundant in UK waters and is packed with omega-3s. It can be grilled, baked, or smoked, making it a versatile choice for many Mediterranean-inspired dishes.
- Herring and Trout: These fish are also rich in omega-3s and are often available fresh from British fisheries. Herring can be pickled

or grilled, while trout is delicious when baked with herbs and lemon.
- Shellfish: The UK is known for its excellent shellfish, including mussels, scallops, and crabs. These can be easily incorporated into Mediterranean-style dishes, such as seafood stews or pasta with shellfish.

4. **Olive Oil and Healthy Fats:**
- Olive oil is a signature ingredient in the Mediterranean diet, known for its heart-healthy monounsaturated fats and robust flavour. While high-quality olive oil is widely available in the UK, it can be more expensive than other cooking oils. To adapt, consider using a blend of olive oil and locally produced rapeseed oil, which also contains healthy fats and is more affordable. Rapeseed oil has a mild flavour and a high smoke point, making it suitable for cooking and baking.
- For a purely Mediterranean experience, reserve extra virgin olive oil for drizzling over salads, vegetables, and finished dishes to enjoy its full flavour and health benefits.

HOW TO CHOOSE FRESH, QUALITY INGREDIENTS IN BRITISH SUPERMARKETS

One of the key aspects of the Mediterranean diet is the emphasis on fresh, high-quality ingredients. Here's how to navigate British supermarkets to ensure you're selecting the best produce, proteins, and pantry staples for your Mediterranean-inspired meals:

1. **Shopping for Fresh Produce:**
- Seasonal Shopping: Always aim to buy fruits and vegetables that are in season. Seasonal produce is not only fresher and more flavourful but also tends to be more affordable and environmentally friendly. Many British supermarkets and local markets offer seasonal guides or labels that indicate when a product is at its peak.
- Organic and Local Options: Where possible, choose organic produce, especially for items like leafy greens, berries, and apples, which are more susceptible to pesticide residues. Additionally, look for produce that is grown locally, as it often reaches the shelves sooner after harvesting, ensuring better freshness and nutritional content.
- Visual and Tactile Cues: When selecting fresh produce, use your senses. Fruits and vegetables should be vibrant in colour, free from blemishes, and firm to the touch (with the exception of naturally softer items like ripe tomatoes or avocados). Avoid produce that is bruised, wilted, or has soft spots, as these are signs of deterioration.

2. **Selecting Fish and Seafood:**
- Freshness Indicators: When buying fresh fish, look for clear, bright eyes, shiny scales, and a clean, briny smell. The flesh should be firm and spring back when pressed. If you're buying shellfish, such as mussels or clams, they should be tightly closed or close quickly when tapped—this indicates they are still alive and fresh.
- Sustainability: Opt for sustainably sourced fish whenever possible. Look for labels such as the Marine Stewardship Council (MSC) certification, which indicates that the fish has been caught in an environmentally responsible manner. Many British supermarkets now carry a range of sustainably sourced seafood, making it easier to enjoy the health benefits of fish while supporting sustainable practices.

3. **Choosing Quality Olive Oil:**
- Extra Virgin Olive Oil: For the best flavour and nutritional benefits, choose extra virgin olive oil. This type of olive oil is made from the first pressing of olives and is unrefined, preserving its rich flavour and antioxidants. When shopping, look for bottles that are dark-coloured or opaque, as this protects the oil from light exposure, which can cause it to degrade. Additionally, check the harvest date if available, and aim to purchase oil that is no more than a year old for optimal freshness.
- Storing Olive Oil: Once purchased, store olive oil in a cool, dark place, such as a pantry, to maintain its quality. Avoid storing it near the stove or in direct sunlight, as heat and light can cause the oil to spoil more quickly.

4. **Legumes and Whole Grains:**
   - Quality Considerations: When buying dried legumes and grains, look for products that are free from dust, cracks, and signs of moisture in the packaging. Choose whole grains over refined grains to maximise nutritional benefits. Whole grains should have a firm texture and a slightly nutty aroma, while dried legumes should be uniform in size and colour.
   - Buying in Bulk: Consider purchasing legumes and grains in bulk, especially if you use them frequently. Bulk buying can be more cost-effective, and it allows you to inspect the quality of the product more closely before purchasing.

TIPS FOR SUBSTITUTING HARD-TO-FIND INGREDIENTS WITH LOCAL ALTERNATIVES

Sometimes, Mediterranean recipes call for specific ingredients that may be difficult to find in the UK. However, with a little creativity, you can substitute these with local alternatives that are readily available and still provide similar flavours and textures.

1. **Substituting Fresh Herbs:**
Mediterranean cuisine often relies on herbs like basil, oregano, and rosemary. If these are not available, or if you want to use local herbs, consider:

- Basil: Substitute with fresh parsley or mint, which are commonly available and can add a fresh, vibrant note to dishes.
- Oregano: Replace with thyme or marjoram, which offer a similar earthy flavour and are widely grown in the UK.
- Rosemary: If rosemary is not available, sage can be a good substitute, providing a robust, slightly peppery flavour that complements roasted meats and vegetables.

2. **Replacing Mediterranean Vegetables:**
If you can't find certain Mediterranean vegetables like aubergines or artichokes, try these alternatives:

- Aubergine: Substitute with courgettes (zucchini) or portobello mushrooms. Both have a meaty texture and can be grilled, roasted, or used in stews.
- Artichokes: Replace with asparagus or leeks. These vegetables have a similar slightly bitter flavour and can be steamed, grilled, or used in salads and pasta dishes.

3. **Alternative Grains and Legumes:**
Traditional Mediterranean grains like farro or freekeh may be hard to find. Instead, use:

- Farro: Substitute with barley or spelt, which have a similar chewy texture and nutty flavour.
- Freekeh: Replace with bulgur wheat or quinoa, both of which are commonly available in the UK and can be used in salads, pilafs, or as a side dish.

4. **Finding Fish Substitutes:**
If specific Mediterranean fish like sardines or anchovies are unavailable, try these:

- Sardines: Replace with mackerel or herring, which are rich in omega-3s and have a similarly strong flavour.
- Anchovies: Substitute with capers or Worcestershire sauce to replicate the salty, umami flavour that anchovies provide in dishes like Caesar salad or pasta sauces.

5. **Replacing Mediterranean Cheeses:**
Some Mediterranean cheeses like feta or halloumi might not always be available, but you can use these alternatives:

- Feta: Substitute with crumbled goat cheese or Ricotta Salata. Both have a similar tangy, crumbly texture.
- Halloumi: Replace with grilled paneer or Cypriot-style cheese. These cheeses can be grilled or fried and offer a similar texture and mild flavour.

By making these substitutions and focusing on the quality of the ingredients you use, it's possible to fully embrace the Mediterranean diet in the UK, enjoying both its flavours and its health benefits without needing to rely solely on imported ingredients.

In summary, adapting the Mediterranean diet to the UK context is not only possible but can be highly rewarding. By making thoughtful substitutions and focusing on local, seasonal produce, you can enjoy the full range of benefits that this diet offers while supporting British agriculture and making the most of what is available in local markets and supermarkets. This approach ensures that the Mediterranean diet is not just a set of guidelines but a practical, sustainable way of eating that fits seamlessly into your life in the UK.

5. Guide to the 30-Day Meal Plan

The 30-day meal plan is a practical tool designed to help you seamlessly incorporate the Mediterranean diet into your daily life. Whether you're new to this dietary approach or looking to deepen your commitment, this plan provides structure and guidance to ensure that your meals are balanced, nutritious, and aligned with the principles of the Mediterranean lifestyle. In this section, we'll explore how to use the meal plan effectively, the benefits of following a structured plan, and how to personalize it to meet different dietary needs.

HOW TO USE THE MEAL PLAN: TIPS FOR MEAL PREP AND WEEKLY PLANNING

The key to successfully following a 30-day meal plan lies in thoughtful preparation and planning. By taking the time to organise your meals ahead of time, you can simplify your cooking process, reduce food waste, and ensure that you're always prepared with healthy, delicious meals. Here are some tips to help you make the most of your meal plan:

1. **Weekly Planning:**
- Set Aside Time for Planning: At the start of each week, take 30 minutes to review the upcoming meals in your 30-day plan. Consider your schedule and any social or family commitments that might affect your meal times. Use this opportunity to adjust the plan as needed, ensuring it fits your lifestyle.
- Create a Shopping List: Once you've reviewed the meals for the week, create a comprehensive shopping list that includes all the ingredients you'll need. Organise your list by sections of the supermarket (e.g., produce, dairy, pantry items) to

streamline your shopping experience. This will save you time and reduce the likelihood of forgetting essential ingredients.
- Incorporate Seasonal Produce: Whenever possible, try to select seasonal and locally-sourced produce. Not only is this more sustainable, but it also ensures that your meals are fresh and flavourful. If certain items are out of season, make adjustments to the plan by substituting with similar ingredients that are readily available.

2. **Meal Prep:**
- Batch Cooking: One of the most effective ways to save time and ensure you stick to your meal plan is through batch cooking. Choose a day (such as Sunday) to prepare large quantities of staple ingredients like grains, legumes, and roasted vegetables. These can be stored in the refrigerator and used throughout the week in various meals.
- Prep Ingredients in Advance: To make weekday cooking quicker and easier, consider prepping ingredients ahead of time. Wash and chop vegetables, marinate proteins, and pre-cook grains like quinoa or brown rice. Store these prepped ingredients in airtight containers so that they're ready to use when it's time to cook.
- Portion Control: Invest in a set of quality containers that can be used to store individual portions of meals. This makes it easy to grab a healthy lunch or dinner on busy days and helps with portion control, ensuring you stick to appropriate serving sizes.

3. **Flexible Cooking:**
- Plan for Leftovers: Intentionally cook extra portions for certain meals that can be enjoyed as leftovers the next day. This not only saves time but also reduces food waste. For example, a large batch of vegetable stew can be served for dinner one night and then reheated for lunch the next day.
- Mix and Match: The meal plan should serve as a guide rather than a rigid set of rules. Feel free to mix and match recipes based on what you have on hand or what you're in the mood for. If you're craving a particular dish, adjust the plan accordingly. The key is to maintain the balance of nutrients that the Mediterranean diet promotes.

THE BENEFITS OF FOLLOWING A STRUCTURED PLAN: REDUCING STRESS AND IMPROVING EATING HABITS

Following a structured 30-day meal plan offers several benefits that extend beyond the immediate convenience of knowing what's for dinner each night. Here's how a structured plan can enhance your overall well-being:

1. **Reducing Decision Fatigue:**
- One of the most significant benefits of a structured meal plan is that it reduces decision fatigue. In our daily lives, we are often faced with countless decisions, and deciding what to eat can become a source of stress, particularly when trying to maintain a healthy diet. By following a meal plan, you eliminate the need to make last-minute decisions about what to cook or eat, which can help reduce stress and free up mental energy for other tasks.

2. **Promoting Consistency and Healthy Habits:**
- A structured meal plan encourages consistency in your eating habits. By having a clear guide to follow, you're more likely to stick to your dietary goals, whether that's eating more vegetables, reducing sugar intake, or ensuring balanced meals. Consistency is key to developing and maintaining healthy habits over the long term, and a meal plan provides the framework needed to achieve this.
- Over time, following a meal plan can help you internalise healthy eating patterns, making it easier to maintain these habits even after the 30 days are over. This can lead to lasting improvements in your diet and overall health.

3. **Saving Time and Reducing Waste:**
- Planning your meals in advance helps you use your time more efficiently, both in the kitchen and at the supermarket. With a clear plan in place, you can streamline your shopping trips, reduce the number of spontaneous or unnecessary purchases, and ensure that you have everything you need for the week.
- By cooking at home and following a meal

plan, you're also less likely to waste food. The plan helps you use up all the ingredients you purchase, as each meal is designed to incorporate a variety of fresh produce and pantry staples. This not only saves money but also supports a more sustainable lifestyle by reducing food waste.

4. **Enhancing Nutritional Balance:**
- A well-structured meal plan ensures that you're getting a balanced intake of nutrients across your meals. The Mediterranean diet, in particular, focuses on a variety of whole foods that provide essential vitamins, minerals, and healthy fats. By following a plan, you can ensure that your diet is nutritionally complete, helping to support your energy levels, immune system, and overall health.
- The plan also helps you avoid common pitfalls, such as skipping meals or reaching for less healthy convenience foods when time is tight. With nutritious meals already planned and prepped, you're more likely to make healthier choices consistently.

PERSONALIZING THE MEAL PLAN FOR DIFFERENT DIETARY NEEDS (GLUTEN-FREE, VEGETARIAN, ETC.)

The Mediterranean diet is inherently flexible, making it easy to adapt the 30-day meal plan to accommodate different dietary needs and preferences. Here's how you can personalise the plan for specific diets, ensuring that it remains inclusive and accessible to everyone:

1. **Gluten-Free:**
- Grains and Starches: For those following a gluten-free diet, substitute traditional grains like wheat, barley, and farro with gluten-free alternatives such as quinoa, brown rice, millet, and gluten-free oats. These grains still provide the fibre and nutrients essential to the Mediterranean diet without the gluten.
- Bread and Pasta: Opt for gluten-free bread and pasta, which are now widely available in most supermarkets. Look for varieties made from rice, corn, quinoa, or chickpeas, which align with the principles of the Mediterranean diet and provide similar texture and taste.
- Label Reading: Always check labels for hidden sources of gluten, particularly in processed foods, sauces, and condiments. When in doubt, choose fresh, whole foods that are naturally gluten-free.

2. **Vegetarian:**
- Protein Sources: The Mediterranean diet already places a strong emphasis on plant-based foods, making it easy to adapt for a vegetarian lifestyle. Legumes, such as lentils, chickpeas, and beans, serve as excellent protein sources and can be featured in a variety of dishes, from soups and stews to salads and grain bowls.
- Eggs and Dairy: Incorporate eggs and dairy products like Greek yogurt and cheese for additional protein. These can be used in meals like frittatas, yogurt bowls, or as toppings for salads and roasted vegetables.
- Meat Substitutes: If desired, use meat substitutes such as tofu, tempeh, or seitan in place of animal proteins in certain recipes. These options provide a similar texture and can absorb the flavours of Mediterranean herbs and spices, making them a versatile addition to vegetarian meals.

3. **Vegan:**
- Eliminating Animal Products: For a vegan adaptation, eliminate all animal products, including meat, fish, dairy, and eggs. Replace them with plant-based proteins like legumes, nuts, seeds, and tofu.
- Dairy Substitutes: Use plant-based dairy alternatives, such as almond or oat milk, in place of cow's milk. Coconut yogurt or almond-based cheese can be used as substitutes for traditional dairy products in recipes.
- Omega-3 Sources: Since fish is a primary source of omega-3 fatty acids in the Mediterranean diet, vegans can incorporate flaxseeds, chia seeds, walnuts, and algae-based supplements to ensure adequate intake of these essential fats.

4. **Low-Carb:**
- Reducing Carbohydrate Intake: For those following a low-carb version of the Mediterranean diet, focus on non-starchy

vegetables, lean proteins, and healthy fats. Reduce the intake of grains, legumes, and starchy vegetables.
- Vegetable Substitutes: Use vegetables like cauliflower and courgette as substitutes for higher-carb foods. For example, cauliflower rice can replace traditional rice, and courgette noodles (zoodles) can be used in place of pasta.
- Healthy Fats: Emphasize healthy fats from sources like olive oil, avocados, nuts, and seeds. These foods provide energy and satiety while keeping carbohydrate intake low.

5. **Pescatarian:**
- Emphasizing Seafood: A pescatarian adaptation of the Mediterranean diet focuses on fish and seafood as the primary sources of protein. Include a variety of fish, such as salmon, mackerel, and sardines, which are rich in omega-3 fatty acids and align with the diet's principles.
- Complementary Plant-Based Foods: Pair seafood with a wide array of plant-based foods, including vegetables, legumes, and whole grains. This combination ensures a balanced intake of protein, fibre, and healthy fats.
- Dairy and Eggs: Continue to include dairy and eggs if they are part of your pescatarian diet, using them to round out meals with additional protein and calcium.

In conclusion, the 30-day meal plan is a powerful tool for integrating the Mediterranean diet into your daily life. By following the tips for meal prep and planning, you can simplify your cooking routine, reduce stress, and establish healthier eating habits. The flexibility of the plan allows for easy personalization, ensuring that it meets the diverse needs of individuals with different dietary preferences and requirements. With thoughtful planning and adaptation, the 30-day meal plan can become the foundation for a sustainable and enjoyable way of eating that supports long-term health and well-being.

At the end of this book, you'll find a carefully structured 30-day meal plan that has been optimally designed using the recipes featured throughout these pages. This meal plan is tailored to help you seamlessly integrate the Mediterranean diet into your daily routine, ensuring that each meal is balanced, nutritious, and delicious. Whether you're just starting out or looking to deepen your commitment to a healthier lifestyle, this meal plan provides a practical guide to making the most of the recipes within this book.

6. The Philosophy of "Eating Well"

The Mediterranean diet is much more than a set of dietary guidelines; it represents a holistic approach to food and lifestyle that prioritises not only what you eat but also how you eat. This philosophy of "eating well" is deeply rooted in mindful eating, balanced nutrition, and the broader Mediterranean lifestyle, all of which contribute to overall well-being. In this section, we'll explore the importance of mindful eating, how the Mediterranean diet encourages a balanced approach to nutrition, and the profound impact of the Mediterranean lifestyle on health and happiness.

THE IMPORTANCE OF MINDFUL EATING: EATING WITH INTENTION AND PLEASURE

Mindful eating is a central tenet of the Mediterranean philosophy of "eating well." It involves paying full attention to the experience of eating, appreciating the flavours, textures, and aromas of food, and being present in the moment. This practice not only enhances the enjoyment of food but also promotes better digestion, satisfaction, and overall health.

1. **Eating with Intention:**
- Mindful eating begins with the intention to nourish your body and mind. It encourages you to approach each meal with a sense of purpose, choosing foods that support your health and well-being. In the context of the Mediterranean diet, this means selecting fresh, wholesome ingredients that are rich in nutrients and minimally processed.
- By eating with intention, you become more aware of your hunger and satiety cues, helping you to eat in alignment with your body's needs rather than out of habit or emotion. This intentional approach to eating can lead to healthier food choices and a more balanced diet over time.

2. **Savouring the Experience:**
- The Mediterranean diet celebrates the sensory pleasures of food. Meals are meant to be savoured slowly, allowing you to fully experience the flavours, textures, and aromas of each dish. This slow, deliberate approach to eating not only enhances the enjoyment of food but also aids in digestion and prevents overeating.
- Taking the time to savour your food can also foster a deeper appreciation for the quality and craftsmanship that goes into preparing a meal. Whether it's a simple salad drizzled with olive oil or a complex seafood stew, each dish is an opportunity to connect with the rich culinary traditions of the Mediterranean.

3. **Mindful Eating Practices:**
- To practice mindful eating, start by eliminating distractions during meals. Turn off the television, put away your phone, and focus on the food in front of you. Pay attention to the colours, shapes, and smells of your meal before taking the first bite.
- As you eat, chew slowly and thoroughly, noticing the different flavours and textures as they unfold in your mouth. Take small pauses between bites to check in with your body and assess whether you're still hungry or beginning to feel full.
- Mindful eating also involves being aware of the emotional aspects of eating. Recognise when you're eating for reasons other than hunger, such as stress or boredom, and try to address those emotions in healthier ways. By being mindful of your eating habits, you can develop a more positive and balanced relationship with food.

HOW THE MEDITERRANEAN DIET ENCOURAGES A BALANCED APPROACH TO NUTRITION

The Mediterranean diet is a model of balanced nutrition, providing a wide array of nutrients that support health and vitality. It emphasises variety, moderation, and the consumption of whole, natural foods, all of which contribute to a well-rounded and sustainable way of eating.

1. **Variety and Nutritional Diversity:**
- One of the hallmarks of the Mediterranean diet is its emphasis on variety. By incorporating a wide range of fruits, vegetables, whole grains, legumes, nuts, seeds, fish, and healthy fats, the diet ensures that you receive a broad spectrum of essential nutrients.
- This diversity not only prevents dietary monotony but also reduces the risk of nutrient deficiencies. For example, the regular consumption of different coloured fruits and vegetables provides a rich supply of vitamins, minerals, and antioxidants, each offering unique health benefits. Similarly, including a variety of protein sources, such as fish, legumes, and dairy, ensures adequate intake of essential amino acids, omega-3 fatty acids, and calcium.

2. **Moderation and Portion Control:**
- The Mediterranean diet encourages moderation in all things, particularly when it comes to portion sizes and the consumption of certain foods like meat, sweets, and alcohol. This balanced approach helps to maintain a healthy weight and reduces the risk of overeating.
- Rather than eliminating food groups, the Mediterranean diet focuses on portion control and mindful eating practices. For instance, red meat is consumed sparingly, often as a small part of a larger dish rather than the main focus of the meal. Sweets and desserts are enjoyed occasionally, with an emphasis on fresh fruit as a naturally sweet alternative.
- Alcohol, particularly wine, is consumed in moderation, usually during meals and in social settings. This moderate consumption, combined with a nutrient-dense diet, supports overall health and well-being without the negative effects associated with excessive drinking.

3. **Whole Foods Over Processed Foods:**
- A key principle of the Mediterranean diet is the preference for whole, minimally processed foods over highly processed options. Whole foods retain their natural nutrient content and are free from added sugars, unhealthy fats, and artificial additives, making them a healthier choice.
- This focus on whole foods not only enhances the nutritional quality of your diet but also encourages the consumption of foods that are closer to their natural state, such as fresh vegetables, whole grains, and cold-pressed olive oil. By choosing whole foods, you're more likely to consume a diet that is rich in fibre, vitamins, and antioxidants, all of which are essential for maintaining good health.

THE IMPACT OF THE MEDITERRANEAN LIFESTYLE ON OVERALL WELL-BEING

The Mediterranean diet is part of a broader lifestyle that encompasses not only food choices but also physical activity, social connections, and a positive approach to life. This holistic lifestyle is central to the Mediterranean way of "eating well" and contributes significantly to overall well-being.

1. **Physical Activity:**
- Regular physical activity is an integral part of the Mediterranean lifestyle. In Mediterranean cultures, physical activity is often incorporated into daily life through walking, gardening, and other forms of low-intensity exercise. This natural movement helps to maintain physical health, reduce the risk of chronic diseases, and enhance mental well-being.
- The combination of a nutrient-rich diet and regular physical activity supports a healthy weight, strong muscles and bones, and a lower risk of conditions such as heart disease, diabetes, and osteoporosis. Moreover, physical activity is known to improve mood, reduce stress, and boost overall energy levels, further enhancing the quality of life.

2. **Social Connections and Community:**
- The Mediterranean diet is deeply rooted in social and communal eating practices. Meals are often shared with family and friends, and the act of eating together is

seen as an important time for connection and celebration.
- This emphasis on social dining promotes emotional well-being by fostering a sense of belonging and reducing feelings of loneliness and isolation. Research has shown that strong social connections are linked to longer life expectancy, better mental health, and a greater sense of purpose and happiness.
- The Mediterranean approach to communal meals also encourages mindful eating and moderation, as shared dishes are often enjoyed slowly over the course of a meal, allowing for better digestion and more meaningful conversations.

3. **Positive Outlook and Enjoyment of Life:**
- A positive outlook and the enjoyment of life are central to the Mediterranean lifestyle. This approach is reflected in the way food is celebrated as one of life's pleasures, with an emphasis on fresh, flavourful, and satisfying meals.
- The Mediterranean lifestyle encourages taking time to appreciate the simple pleasures in life, whether it's enjoying a leisurely meal, spending time outdoors, or connecting with loved ones. This positive approach to life is associated with lower stress levels, improved mental health, and a greater sense of well-being.
- The diet itself, rich in nutrients that support brain health and reduce inflammation, further contributes to mental well-being. Foods high in omega-3 fatty acids, antioxidants, and vitamins, such as fish, olive oil, nuts, and leafy greens, have been shown to protect against cognitive decline and improve mood, making the Mediterranean diet a powerful ally in promoting both physical and mental health.

In conclusion, the philosophy of "eating well" within the Mediterranean diet extends beyond the food on your plate. It encompasses a mindful approach to eating, a balanced and varied diet, and a lifestyle that prioritises physical activity, social connections, and a positive outlook on life. By embracing this philosophy, you can experience not only the health benefits of the Mediterranean diet but also a richer, more fulfilling relationship with food and life itself. This holistic approach to well-being is what makes the Mediterranean diet truly unique and effective in supporting long-term health and happiness.

7. Tools and Accessories for Mediterranean Cooking

Mediterranean cooking is known for its simplicity, freshness, and the use of high-quality ingredients. To fully embrace this style of cooking, it's important to have the right tools and accessories in your kitchen. These tools not only make the preparation of Mediterranean dishes easier but also enhance the overall cooking experience. In this section, we'll explore the essential utensils for preparing Mediterranean dishes, offer tips for organizing your kitchen and storing ingredients, and provide suggestions for cooking efficiently and stress-free.

ESSENTIAL UTENSILS FOR PREPARING MEDITERRANEAN DISHES

Having the right utensils can make a significant difference in your ability to prepare Mediterranean dishes with ease and enjoyment. Here are some of the most essential tools you should have in your kitchen:

1. **Chef's Knife:**
- A high-quality chef's knife is arguably the most important tool in any kitchen, especially when it comes to Mediterranean cooking, where fresh vegetables, herbs, and meats are frequently chopped, sliced, and diced. A sharp, well-balanced chef's knife allows you to prepare ingredients quickly and with precision, making it easier to create everything from finely chopped salads to neatly sliced meats and vegetables.

2. **Cutting Boards:**
- Invest in a set of good cutting boards—preferably one for vegetables, one for fruits, and one for meats—to avoid cross-contamination. Wooden or bamboo cutting boards are ideal for vegetables and herbs, as they are gentle on knives and have natural antibacterial properties. A sturdy plastic cutting board can be reserved for meats, which can be easily sanitized after use.

3. **Mortar and Pestle:**
- A mortar and pestle is an essential tool for grinding spices, crushing garlic, and making traditional Mediterranean condiments like pesto or tapenade. While electric grinders are available, the manual process of using a mortar and pestle helps to release the natural oils in herbs and spices, resulting in more aromatic and flavourful dishes.

4. **Olive Oil Dispenser:**
- Olive oil is a cornerstone of Mediterranean cooking, and having a dedicated dispenser for it can make cooking more convenient. A glass or ceramic olive oil dispenser with a spout allows you to drizzle oil evenly over dishes or into a pan without overpouring. This not only enhances the flavour of your dishes but also helps with portion control.

5. **Cast Iron Skillet:**
- A cast iron skillet is a versatile and durable tool perfect for Mediterranean cooking. It can be used for searing meats, sautéing vegetables, and even baking bread. Cast iron retains heat well, ensuring even cooking, and when properly seasoned, it adds a natural non-stick surface that enhances the flavour of your food.

6. **Non-Stick Frying Pan:**
- While a cast iron skillet is excellent for many tasks, a non-stick frying pan is essential for cooking delicate items like fish, eggs, and pancakes. Choose a high-quality non-stick pan that distributes heat evenly and is easy to clean, which will save you time during meal preparation.

7. **Zester or Microplane:**
- A zester or microplane is a small, yet incredibly useful tool for adding a burst of citrus flavour to your dishes. In Mediterranean cooking, lemon zest is frequently used to brighten up salads, pasta, and fish dishes. A microplane can also be used to grate hard cheeses like Parmesan or Pecorino Romano.

8. **Salad Spinner:**
- A zester or microplane is a small, yet

incredibly useful tool for adding a burst of citrus flavour to your dishes. In Mediterranean cooking, lemon zest is frequently used to brighten up salads, pasta, and fish dishes. A microplane can also be used to grate hard cheeses like Parmesan or Pecorino Romano.

9. **Dutch Oven or Large Cooking Pot:**
- A Dutch oven or a large, heavy-bottomed cooking pot is ideal for making soups, stews, and braised dishes. These pots retain heat well and cook food evenly, making them perfect for slow-cooking dishes that are rich in flavour, such as Mediterranean stews and braised meats.

10. **Mandoline Slicer:**
- A mandoline slicer is a useful tool for quickly and uniformly slicing vegetables, which is particularly handy for preparing dishes like ratatouille or thinly sliced salads. It allows you to achieve precise cuts that are difficult to replicate with a knife alone.

11. **Wooden Spoons and Spatulas:**
- Wooden spoons and spatulas are gentle on your cookware and perfect for stirring, sautéing, and serving. They are heat-resistant and do not react with acidic ingredients like tomatoes, making them ideal for Mediterranean cooking.

12. **Grill Pan:**
- A grill pan is useful for creating those characteristic grill marks on vegetables, fish, and meats, which are often grilled in Mediterranean cuisine. It allows you to achieve the flavour of outdoor grilling right on your stovetop.

TIPS FOR ORGANIZING THE KITCHEN AND STORING INGREDIENTS

An organized kitchen is the foundation of efficient cooking. By setting up your kitchen in a way that supports the Mediterranean style of cooking, you can streamline your meal preparation process and ensure that your ingredients are fresh and easily accessible.

1. **Create Zones in Your Kitchen:**
- Organize your kitchen into zones based on different activities, such as prep work, cooking, and storage. Keep your most frequently used tools and ingredients within easy reach in each zone. For example, store knives, cutting boards, and mixing bowls near your prep area, while pots, pans, and utensils should be close to the stove.

2. **Keep Your Pantry Well-Stocked:**
- A well-stocked pantry is essential for Mediterranean cooking, where fresh and dried herbs, grains, legumes, and canned goods play a significant role. Organize your pantry by grouping similar items together, such as grains in one section, canned goods in another, and spices in a separate area. Use clear, airtight containers to store grains, nuts, and seeds, which will keep them fresh and allow you to see when it's time to restock.

3. **Store Fresh Ingredients Properly:**
- Proper storage of fresh ingredients is key to maintaining their quality and flavour. Store fresh herbs like parsley, cilantro, and mint in the refrigerator, wrapped in a damp paper towel and placed in a plastic bag or container. For longer storage, consider freezing herbs in olive oil using an ice cube tray, so you can easily add them to dishes as needed.
- Vegetables should be stored in the crisper drawer of your refrigerator to maintain their freshness. Root vegetables like potatoes and onions should be stored in a cool, dark place, away from direct sunlight, to prevent sprouting.

4. **Utilize Vertical Space:**
- Maximize storage space in your kitchen by using wall-mounted racks or shelves to store pots, pans, and utensils. Magnetic strips can be installed to hold knives, freeing up drawer space and keeping your most important tools within easy reach.

5. **Label and Date Stored Items:**
- When storing leftovers, prepped ingredients, or pantry items, make sure to label and date them. This practice helps you keep track of what needs to be used first and reduces food waste. It's also a good idea to rotate items in your pantry and fridge regularly, placing newer items behind older ones to ensure they are used in a timely manner.

6. **Organize Spices and Oils:**
- Spices and oils are central to Mediterranean cooking, so keep them organized and easily accessible. Store spices in a cool, dark place, such as a drawer or cabinet away from the stove, to preserve their flavour. Use a spice rack or drawer organizer to keep them arranged alphabetically or by cuisine. Oils should be stored in a dark, cool cupboard to prevent them from going rancid.

SUGGESTIONS FOR COOKING EFFICIENTLY AND STRESS-FREE

Mediterranean cooking is all about enjoying the process of preparing and sharing food. However, it's important to approach cooking in a way that minimizes stress and maximizes efficiency. Here are some tips to help you cook Mediterranean dishes with ease and confidence:

1. **Plan Ahead:**
- Planning your meals and prepping ingredients in advance can significantly reduce the time and stress associated with cooking. As mentioned in the meal plan section, taking time each week to plan your meals and prepare ingredients like chopping vegetables, marinating meats, or cooking grains will make the actual cooking process faster and more enjoyable.
- Additionally, keep a list of go-to recipes that you can easily pull together on busy days. These might include simple pasta dishes, salads, or grilled meats that require minimal preparation but are still packed with flavour.

2. **Cook in Batches:**
- Batch cooking is a great way to save time during the week. Prepare large quantities of staples like roasted vegetables, grains, and legumes, and store them in the refrigerator or freezer. These pre-cooked ingredients can then be mixed and matched throughout the week to create different meals with minimal effort.

3. **Embrace One-Pot Meals:**
- One-pot meals, such as soups, stews, and casseroles, are not only comforting but also incredibly efficient. They require less cleanup and allow you to cook a complete meal in a single pot or pan. Mediterranean dishes like ratatouille, minestrone, and chicken cacciatore are excellent examples of one-pot meals that are both delicious and easy to prepare.

4. **Keep It Simple:**
- Mediterranean cooking emphasizes simplicity, so don't feel pressured to create elaborate meals every day. Focus on using high-quality ingredients and letting their natural flavours shine. A simple salad with fresh tomatoes, cucumbers, and feta cheese, drizzled with olive oil and lemon juice, can be just as satisfying as a more complex dish.

5. **Use Your Freezer Wisely:**
- Your freezer can be a powerful tool for stress-free cooking. Freeze homemade broths, sauces, and pestos in small portions so you can easily add them to dishes as needed. You can also freeze leftovers for quick meals on busy days. Just be sure to label and date everything to keep your freezer organized.

6. **Clean as You Go:**
- To avoid a daunting cleanup after cooking, practice cleaning as you go. Wash dishes, utensils, and cutting boards immediately after using them, and wipe down counters while waiting for something to cook. This not only keeps your kitchen tidy but also makes the cooking process more enjoyable.

7. **Stay Flexible:**
- Mediterranean cooking encourages creativity and flexibility. Don't be afraid to improvise with the ingredients you have on hand. If you're missing an ingredient, think about what might work as a substitute. The ability to adapt recipes based on what's available will make cooking less stressful and more fun.

In conclusion, having the right tools and organizing your kitchen effectively are key components of successful Mediterranean cooking. By equipping your kitchen with essential utensils, organizing your space to support efficient meal preparation, and adopting strategies to cook stress-free, you can fully enjoy the process of creating delicious and nutritious Mediterranean dishes. This approach not only enhances your cooking experience but also aligns with the broader Mediterranean philosophy of enjoying food and life in a balanced, mindful way.

8. Frequently Asked Questions About the Mediterranean Diet

The Mediterranean diet is widely celebrated for its health benefits, delicious flavors, and sustainable approach to eating. However, like any dietary pattern, it can raise questions, especially for those who are new to it or looking to deepen their understanding. In this section, we will address some of the most common questions about the Mediterranean diet, offer guidance on how to manage eating out while following the diet, and debunk some common myths and misconceptions that may arise.

ANSWERS TO THE MOST COMMON QUESTIONS ABOUT THE MEDITERRANEAN DIET

1. **What Exactly Is the Mediterranean Diet?**
- The Mediterranean diet is a way of eating that is inspired by the traditional dietary patterns of the countries bordering the Mediterranean Sea, particularly Greece, Italy, Spain, and southern France. It emphasizes whole, minimally processed foods, including fruits, vegetables, whole grains, legumes, nuts, seeds, fish, and olive oil. The diet also includes moderate amounts of dairy, particularly cheese and yogurt, and wine, typically consumed with meals. Red meat and sweets are consumed sparingly.
1. The Mediterranean diet is not just about food; it also promotes a lifestyle that includes regular physical activity, social connections, and mindful eating practices. This holistic approach contributes to its reputation as one of the healthiest diets in the world.
2. **Is the Mediterranean Diet Suitable for Everyone?**
- Yes, the Mediterranean diet is suitable for most people, regardless of age or health

status. Its emphasis on balanced, nutrient-rich foods makes it an excellent choice for those looking to improve their overall health, manage weight, or prevent chronic diseases. It can also be easily adapted to meet specific dietary needs, such as gluten-free, vegetarian, or vegan diets.
- However, as with any diet, it's important to consider individual health conditions and nutritional requirements. If you have specific health concerns or dietary restrictions, it may be helpful to consult with a healthcare professional or registered dietitian before making significant changes to your eating habits.

3. **How Does the Mediterranean Diet Help with Weight Management?**
- The Mediterranean diet promotes weight management through its emphasis on whole, minimally processed foods that are rich in fiber and healthy fats. These foods help to keep you feeling full and satisfied, reducing the likelihood of overeating or reaching for unhealthy snacks.
- Additionally, the diet's focus on portion control and mindful eating encourages a more balanced approach to food. By consuming a variety of nutrient-dense foods and paying attention to hunger and fullness cues, you're more likely to maintain a healthy weight over time.

4. **Can I Follow the Mediterranean Diet If I Don't Like Fish?**
- Yes, you can still follow the Mediterranean diet even if you don't like fish. While fish is a key component of the diet, particularly for its omega-3 fatty acids, there are plenty of other foods that can provide similar health benefits. For example, you can include plant-based sources of omega-3s, such as flaxseeds, chia seeds, walnuts, and algae-based supplements.
- Additionally, you can focus on other protein sources that are part of the Mediterranean diet, such as legumes, nuts, seeds, eggs, and moderate amounts of dairy. Incorporating a variety of these foods will ensure that your diet remains balanced and nutrient-rich.

5. **How Much Olive Oil Should I Use?**
- Olive oil is a staple of the Mediterranean diet, and it's recommended to use it as your primary cooking oil. While there isn't a strict limit on how much olive oil you should use, it's important to remember that it is still a fat, and therefore calorie-dense. A general guideline is to use about 2 to 4 tablespoons per day, depending on your energy needs and overall dietary intake.
- Olive oil can be used for cooking, drizzling over salads, or as a finishing touch to enhance the flavor of dishes. For the best health benefits, opt for extra virgin olive oil, which is rich in antioxidants and healthy monounsaturated fats.

6. **Is Wine Really Part of the Mediterranean Diet?**
- Yes, moderate consumption of wine, particularly red wine, is a traditional component of the Mediterranean diet. Wine is typically enjoyed with meals and in a social setting, rather than in isolation. The key is moderation—this generally means up to one glass per day for women and up to two glasses per day for men.
- It's important to note that wine is not essential to the health benefits of the Mediterranean diet. If you don't drink alcohol or choose not to include wine in your diet, you can still enjoy all the other benefits of the Mediterranean diet without it.

7. **Can I Follow the Mediterranean Diet on a Budget?**
- Absolutely! While the Mediterranean diet emphasizes fresh, high-quality ingredients, it can be adapted to fit a variety of budgets. Focus on purchasing seasonal and locally-sourced produce, which is often more affordable. Dried legumes, whole grains, and canned fish are also cost-effective staples that are central to the Mediterranean diet.
- Planning your meals in advance, buying in bulk, and minimizing food waste by using leftovers creatively can further help you stick to a budget while enjoying the benefits of the Mediterranean diet.

HOW TO MANAGE EATING OUT WHILE FOLLOWING THE MEDITERRANEAN DIET

Eating out is a common part of modern life, and it's entirely possible to enjoy restaurant meals while staying true to the principles of the Mediterranean diet. Here are some tips for managing eating out:

1. **Choose Mediterranean or Mediterranean-Inspired Restaurants:**
- When possible, opt for restaurants that specialize in Mediterranean cuisine. These establishments are more likely to offer dishes that align with the Mediterranean diet, such as grilled fish, vegetable-based dishes, salads, and whole grain options. Look for items like Greek salads, hummus, grilled vegetables, and seafood dishes, which are typically prepared with olive oil and fresh herbs.

2. **Focus on Whole Foods:**
- When dining out, aim to choose dishes that feature whole, minimally processed foods. Look for menu options that include plenty of vegetables, lean proteins, and healthy fats. For example, opt for a grilled chicken or fish dish served with a side of vegetables or a salad, rather than fried or heavily processed items.
- Avoid dishes that are smothered in creamy sauces or heavily fried, as these are often high in unhealthy fats and calories. Instead, ask for your food to be prepared with olive oil, and request dressings or sauces on the side so you can control the amount used.

3. **Portion Control:**
- Restaurant portions can often be larger than what you would typically serve at home. To manage portion sizes, consider sharing an entrée with a dining companion or ordering a couple of small plates or appetizers instead of a main course. You can also ask for a takeaway box and save half of your meal for later.
- Eating slowly and mindfully will help you recognize when you're full, allowing you to enjoy your meal without overeating. Remember, the Mediterranean diet emphasizes moderation, even when dining out.

4. **Ask Questions:**
- Don't hesitate to ask your server about how a dish is prepared or to request modifications that align with the Mediterranean diet. For example, you might ask for grilled instead of fried options, request extra vegetables, or substitute a side of chips for a salad.
- Many restaurants are happy to accommodate dietary preferences, and being clear about what you want can help you stick to your diet while enjoying a meal out.

5. **Mindful Alcohol Consumption:**
- If you choose to drink alcohol while dining out, follow the Mediterranean diet's guideline of moderation. Opt for a glass of red wine, which complements the flavors of Mediterranean dishes and offers some health benefits. Be mindful of your intake and avoid sugary cocktails or excessive drinking.

MYTHS AND REALITIES ABOUT THE MEDITERRANEAN DIET: DEBUNKING COMMON MISCONCEPTIONS

Despite its popularity, there are several myths and misconceptions surrounding the Mediterranean diet. Here, we'll debunk some of the most common ones to provide a clearer understanding of what the diet truly entails.

1. **Myth: The Mediterranean Diet Is All About Pasta and Pizza**
- Reality: While Italy is part of the Mediterranean region, and pasta and pizza are popular dishes, the Mediterranean diet is much more diverse and balanced. The diet places a greater emphasis on vegetables, fruits, legumes, whole grains, fish, and healthy fats like olive oil. Pasta is enjoyed, but it is typically served in small portions and balanced with plenty of vegetables and lean proteins. Pizza, when consumed, is often made with a thin crust, topped with fresh ingredients, and served as part of a balanced meal.

2. **Myth: The Mediterranean Diet Is High in Fat, So It's Unhealthy**
- Reality: It's true that the Mediterranean diet includes a fair amount of fat, but the majority of this fat comes from healthy sources like olive oil, nuts, and fish. These fats are rich in monounsaturated and polyunsaturated fats, which have been shown to improve heart health by reducing LDL cholesterol levels and providing anti-inflammatory benefits. The diet is not about consuming large amounts of fat indiscriminately; rather, it focuses on the quality and type of fat, which is crucial for overall health.

3. **Myth: You Have to Eat Fish Every Day on the Mediterranean Diet**
- Reality: While fish is an important part of the Mediterranean diet, especially for its omega-3 content, you don't have to eat it every day to follow the diet. The Mediterranean diet is flexible and emphasizes variety. Fish is typically consumed a few times a week, but other protein sources, such as legumes, eggs, and poultry, are also important components of the diet. The key is to include a variety of nutrient-dense foods to meet your nutritional needs.

4. **Myth: The Mediterranean Diet Is Expensive**
- Reality: While some ingredients, like high-quality olive oil or fresh seafood, can be pricey, the Mediterranean diet can be adapted to fit a wide range of budgets. The diet emphasizes affordable staples like legumes, whole grains, seasonal vegetables, and canned fish, which can be purchased in bulk and used in a variety of dishes. Additionally, by planning meals, buying in season, and minimizing food waste, it's possible to enjoy the benefits of the Mediterranean diet without breaking the bank.

5. **Myth: The Mediterranean Diet Is Only for People Who Live in Mediterranean Countries**
- Reality: The principles of the Mediterranean diet can be applied anywhere in the world, not just in Mediterranean countries. While the diet is inspired by the traditional eating patterns of the Mediterranean region, its focus on whole, unprocessed foods, healthy fats, and balanced meals is universal. People in any country can adopt the Mediterranean diet by choosing locally available foods that align with its principles and adapting recipes to suit their cultural and personal preferences.

6. **Myth: The Mediterranean Diet Is a Strict Diet**
- Reality: The Mediterranean diet is not a rigid or prescriptive diet; rather, it is a flexible and sustainable way of eating that can be adapted to individual tastes and lifestyles. There are no strict rules or calorie counting involved. Instead, the diet encourages a focus on whole foods, moderation, and enjoyment of meals. This flexibility makes it easier to maintain over the long term and to adapt to personal and cultural dietary preferences.

In conclusion, the Mediterranean diet is a flexible, sustainable, and health-promoting way of eating that can be adapted to fit a wide range of lifestyles and preferences. By understanding the common questions, learning how to navigate dining out, and debunking common myths, you can fully embrace the Mediterranean diet and enjoy its numerous benefits. This diet is not just about the foods you eat, but also about the way you live, fostering a holistic approach to health and well-being.

9. Conclusion of the Theoretical Section

As we come to the end of the theoretical section, it's important to reflect on the broader significance of the Mediterranean diet—not just as a set of dietary guidelines, but as a holistic lifestyle that can greatly enhance your overall well-being. The Mediterranean diet has gained global recognition for its ability to promote long-term health, prevent chronic diseases, and foster a joyful relationship with food. However, its true power lies in its potential to transform not only what you eat, but how you live, by embracing the values of balance, mindfulness, and community.

FINAL THOUGHTS ON THE IMPORTANCE OF EMBRACING THE MEDITERRANEAN DIET AS A LIFESTYLE

The Mediterranean diet is much more than a diet; it's a way of life that has been cultivated over centuries by the people of the Mediterranean region. This lifestyle is characterised by a deep respect for food, a commitment to quality over quantity, and a profound connection to the land and the seasons. By adopting the Mediterranean diet, you are not just making healthier food choices—you are embracing a lifestyle that prioritises well-being, sustainability, and the joy of eating.

1. **A Lifestyle Rooted in Tradition:**
- The Mediterranean diet is rooted in the traditions of countries like Greece, Italy, Spain, and southern France, where meals are more than just sustenance—they are a time to gather, share, and celebrate life. This sense of community and connection is at the heart of the Mediterranean lifestyle, where food is enjoyed slowly, with gratitude and in good company.
- By embracing this approach, you are not only improving your physical health but also nurturing your mental and emotional well-being. The Mediterranean lifestyle encourages you to take time out of your busy day to enjoy meals, to savour the flavours, and to connect with others—whether that means sharing a meal with family, cooking for friends, or simply taking a moment to appreciate the food on your plate.

2. **Health Benefits Beyond the Plate:**
- The health benefits of the Mediterranean diet extend far beyond the nutrients it provides. This lifestyle promotes physical activity, whether through walking, gardening, or simply being active in daily life. It also encourages a positive relationship with food, where all foods can be enjoyed in moderation, and where no single food group is demonised or excluded.
- By embracing the Mediterranean diet as a lifestyle, you are adopting a holistic approach to health that integrates physical, mental, and social well-being. This balanced way of living can lead to increased longevity, reduced risk of chronic diseases, and a higher quality of life overall.

HOW TO GET STARTED: ENCOURAGEMENT TO EXPERIMENT AND ENJOY COOKING

Starting your journey with the Mediterranean diet doesn't have to be daunting. In fact, one of the greatest joys of this lifestyle is the opportunity to explore new flavours, experiment with different ingredients, and discover the pleasure of cooking and eating well. Here are some tips to help you get started:

1. **Start Small and Build Gradually:**
- If you're new to the Mediterranean diet, start by incorporating small changes into your daily routine. You might begin by adding more fruits and vegetables to your meals, swapping butter for olive oil, or choosing whole grains over refined ones. These small steps can have a big impact on your health and help you ease into the Mediterranean lifestyle without feeling overwhelmed.
- As you become more comfortable with

these changes, you can gradually expand your repertoire by trying new recipes, experimenting with Mediterranean herbs and spices, and exploring different cooking techniques. The key is to take it one step at a time and to enjoy the process of learning and discovering new ways to nourish your body.

2. **Embrace the Joy of Cooking:**
- Cooking is an integral part of the Mediterranean lifestyle, and it's a wonderful way to connect with the food you eat. Don't be afraid to experiment in the kitchen—try out new recipes, play with flavours, and make cooking a creative and enjoyable experience. Whether you're preparing a simple salad or a more elaborate dish, the act of cooking itself can be a form of mindfulness, allowing you to focus on the present moment and take pleasure in the process.
- Remember, the Mediterranean diet is all about simplicity and quality. You don't need to spend hours in the kitchen to create delicious and nutritious meals. Focus on fresh, seasonal ingredients, and let their natural flavours shine through with minimal preparation. This approach not only saves time but also enhances the taste and nutritional value of your meals.

3. **Enjoy the Journey:**
- Transitioning to the Mediterranean diet is not about perfection—it's about progress and finding what works best for you. Give yourself the freedom to explore and experiment, and don't worry about getting everything right from the start. The Mediterranean lifestyle is flexible and adaptable, allowing you to make it your own.
- Celebrate your successes, no matter how small, and enjoy the journey of discovering new foods, flavours, and cooking techniques. Remember that the ultimate goal is to create a sustainable and enjoyable way of eating that enhances your health and happiness.

A PREVIEW OF THE RECIPES THAT FOLLOW AND THEIR CONTRIBUTION TO DAILY WELL-BEING

As you embark on your Mediterranean journey, the following pages of this book are filled with a diverse selection of recipes that will help you incorporate the principles of the Mediterranean diet into your daily life. These recipes are designed to be both delicious and nutritious, making it easy for you to enjoy the benefits of the Mediterranean diet every day.

1. **Balanced and Nutritious Meals:**
- The recipes in this book have been carefully crafted to provide a balance of macronutrients—carbohydrates, proteins, and fats—as well as a rich array of vitamins, minerals, and antioxidants. From hearty breakfasts to satisfying dinners, each recipe is designed to nourish your body and support your overall well-being.
- You'll find a variety of dishes that celebrate the natural flavours of fresh, whole ingredients, with an emphasis on vegetables, fruits, whole grains, legumes, fish, and healthy fats. These meals are not only good for your body but also a joy to eat, reflecting the core philosophy of the Mediterranean diet.

2. **Culinary Exploration and Enjoyment:**
- The recipes in this book invite you to explore the rich culinary traditions of the Mediterranean region. You'll discover classic dishes like Greek salads, Italian pasta, Spanish tapas, and Middle Eastern mezze, as well as modern interpretations that bring new twists to traditional favourites.
- Whether you're a seasoned cook or a beginner in the kitchen, these recipes are designed to be accessible and enjoyable. Clear instructions, simple ingredients, and practical tips make it easy for you to create delicious meals that you and your family will love.

3. **Supporting Long-Term Health:**
- By incorporating these recipes into your daily routine, you'll be taking a proactive step toward improving your long-term health. The Mediterranean diet has been shown to reduce the risk of chronic

diseases, support healthy weight management, and enhance mental and emotional well-being.
- Each meal you prepare from this book is not just a step toward better health, but also a celebration of the pleasure and satisfaction that comes from eating well. As you explore these recipes, you'll find that the Mediterranean diet is not just a diet—it's a way of life that brings joy, flavour, and vitality to your table.

In conclusion, the Mediterranean diet offers a powerful and holistic approach to health and well-being. By embracing this lifestyle, you are not only making healthier food choices but also fostering a deeper connection to the food you eat, the people you share it with, and the world around you. The recipes that follow are your gateway to experiencing the richness of the Mediterranean diet, and they will guide you on a journey toward a healthier, happier, and more fulfilling life.

BREAKFAST

GREEK YOGURT WITH HONEY AND WALNUTS

Prep Time: 5 minutes
Cook Time: None
Difficulty: 1/10
Category: Gluten-Free, Vegetarian

Ingredients:

- 300g Greek yogurt (full-fat or low-fat)
- 2 tbsp honey
- 30g walnuts, roughly chopped

Instructions:

1. Divide the Greek yogurt evenly between two bowls.
2. Drizzle 1 tablespoon of honey over each serving of yogurt.
3. Sprinkle 15g of chopped walnuts on top of each bowl.
4. Serve immediately.

Nutritional Information:
Kcal: 220 | Carb: 25g | Pro: 10g | Fat: 9g | Fib: 1g | Sod: 55mg

MEDITERRANEAN SCRAMBLED EGGS WITH SPINACH AND FETA

Prep Time: 5 minutes
Cook Time: 10 minutes
Difficulty: 2/10
Category: Gluten-Free, Vegetarian

Ingredients:

- 4 large eggs
- 100g spinach, washed
- 50g feta cheese, crumbled
- 1 tbsp olive oil
- Salt and pepper, to taste

Instructions:

1. In a medium bowl, whisk the eggs with a pinch of salt and pepper.
2. Heat the olive oil in a non-stick pan over medium heat.
3. Add the spinach to the pan and cook for 1-2 minutes until wilted.
4. Pour the eggs into the pan, stirring continuously with a spatula.
5. As the eggs begin to set, add the crumbled feta cheese.
6. Continue cooking until the eggs are fully set but still soft, about 3-4 minutes.
7. Serve immediately.

Nutritional Information:
Kcal: 300 | Carb: 3g | Pro: 18g | Fat: 24g | Fib: 2g | Sod: 500mg

AVOCADO TOAST WITH CHERRY TOMATOES AND OLIVE OIL

Prep Time: 5 minutes
Cook Time: None
Difficulty: 1/10
Category: Vegetarian

Ingredients:

- 2 slices whole grain bread
- 1 ripe avocado
- 100g cherry tomatoes, halved
- 1 tbsp extra virgin olive oil
- Salt and pepper, to taste

Instructions:

1. Toast the slices of whole grain bread.
2. While the bread is toasting, mash the avocado in a small bowl with a fork, adding salt and pepper to taste.
3. Spread the mashed avocado evenly over each slice of toast.
4. Top with halved cherry tomatoes and drizzle with olive oil.
5. Serve immediately.

Nutritional Information:
Kcal: 350 | Carb: 35g | Pro: 7g | Fat: 22g | Fib: 10g | Sod: 150mg

OVERNIGHT OATS WITH ALMONDS AND BERRIES

Prep Time: 5 minutes
Cook Time: None (Chill Overnight)
Difficulty: 1/10
Category: Vegetarian

Ingredients:

- 100g rolled oats
- 250ml almond milk (or milk of choice)
- 1 tbsp honey
- 30g almonds, chopped
- 100g mixed berries (strawberries, blueberries, raspberries)

Instructions:

1. In a jar or container, combine the oats, almond milk, and honey. Stir well.
2. Cover and refrigerate overnight.
3. In the morning, top with chopped almonds and mixed berries.
4. Serve cold.

Nutritional Information:
Kcal: 300 | Carb: 45g | Pro: 8g | Fat: 10g | Fib: 7g | Sod: 5mg

TOMATO AND CUCUMBER BREAKFAST SALAD

Prep Time: 5 minutes
Cook Time: None
Difficulty: 1/10
Category: Gluten-Free, Vegetarian, Vegan

Ingredients:

- 200g cherry tomatoes, halved
- 1 cucumber, diced
- 2 tbsp olive oil
- 1 tbsp balsamic vinegar
- Salt and pepper, to taste
- Fresh basil leaves for garnish

Instructions:

1. In a large bowl, combine the cherry tomatoes and cucumber.
2. Drizzle with olive oil and balsamic vinegar.
3. Season with salt and pepper, and toss gently to combine.
4. Garnish with fresh basil leaves and serve.

Nutritional Information:
Kcal: 120 | Carb: 8g | Pro: 2g | Fat: 10g | Fib: 2g | Sod: 20mg

WHOLE GRAIN PORRIDGE WITH FRESH FRUITS AND NUTS

Prep Time: 5 minutes
Cook Time: 10 minutes
Difficulty: 2/10
Category: Vegetarian

Ingredients:

- 80g whole grain oats
- 400ml water or milk
- 1 tbsp honey
- 1 banana, sliced
- 1 handful of mixed nuts (almonds, walnuts, hazelnuts)

Instructions:

1. In a medium saucepan, combine the oats and water (or milk).
2. Bring to a boil, then reduce heat and simmer for 5-7 minutes, stirring occasionally, until the oats are creamy.
3. Stir in the honey and pour into two bowls.
4. Top with sliced banana and mixed nuts.
5. Serve hot.

Nutritional Information:
Kcal: 350 | Carb: 55g | Pro: 10g | Fat: 10g | Fib: 8g | Sod: 10mg

OLIVE OIL AND ORANGE CAKE MUFFINS

Prep Time: 10 minutes
Cook Time: 15 minutes
Difficulty: 3/10
Category: Vegetarian

Ingredients:

- 150g self-raising flour
- 100g caster sugar
- 2 large eggs
- 60ml extra virgin olive oil
- Zest and juice of 1 orange
- 1 tsp vanilla extract
- A pinch of salt

Instructions:

1. Preheat the oven to 180°C (160°C fan) and line a muffin tray with 6 paper cases.
2. In a large bowl, whisk together the eggs, sugar, olive oil, orange zest, orange juice, and vanilla extract.
3. Sift the flour and salt into the wet ingredients, and fold until just combined.
4. Divide the batter evenly among the muffin cases.
5. Bake for 15 minutes, or until a skewer inserted into the centre comes out clean.
6. Let cool before serving.

Nutritional Information (per muffin):
Kcal: 180 | Carb: 25g | Pro: 4g | Fat: 7g | Fib: 1g | Sod: 60mg

MEDITERRANEAN BREAKFAST WRAP WITH EGGS, SPINACH, AND FETA

Prep Time: 5 minutes
Cook Time: 10 minutes
Difficulty: 2/10
Category: Vegetarian

Ingredients:

- 2 large eggs
- 50g spinach, washed
- 50g feta cheese, crumbled
- 2 whole wheat wraps
- 1 tbsp olive oil
- Salt and pepper, to taste

Instructions:

1. In a small bowl, whisk the eggs with salt and pepper.
2. Heat olive oil in a non-stick pan over medium heat.
3. Add the spinach and cook until wilted, about 1-2 minutes.
4. Pour the eggs into the pan, stirring continuously.
5. When the eggs are nearly set, sprinkle the feta cheese over them and continue to cook for another 1-2 minutes.
6. Divide the egg mixture between the two wraps, fold them up, and serve.

Nutritional Information:
Kcal: 350 | Carb: 30g | Pro: 15g | Fat: 20g | Fib: 6g | Sod: 500mg

SAVORY GREEK YOGURT BOWL WITH OLIVES AND CUCUMBERS

Prep Time: 5 minutes
Cook Time: None
Difficulty: 1/10
Category: Gluten-Free, Vegetarian

Ingredients:

- 300g Greek yogurt
- 1 cucumber, diced
- 10 Kalamata olives, pitted and chopped
- 1 tbsp olive oil
- 1 tsp dried oregano
- Salt and pepper, to taste

Instructions:

1. Divide the Greek yogurt evenly between two bowls.
2. Top with diced cucumber and chopped olives.
3. Drizzle with olive oil and sprinkle with oregano, salt, and pepper.
4. Serve immediately.

Nutritional Information:
Kcal: 240 | Carb: 8g | Pro: 12g | Fat: 18g | Fib: 1g | Sod: 600mg

RICOTTA AND HONEY ON WHOLE GRAIN TOAST

Prep Time: 5 minutes
Cook Time: None
Difficulty: 1/10
Category: Vegetarian

Ingredients:

- 2 slices whole grain bread
- 100g ricotta cheese
- 2 tbsp honey
- 1 tsp cinnamon

Instructions:

1. Toast the slices of whole grain bread.
2. Spread 50g of ricotta cheese on each slice.
3. Drizzle 1 tablespoon of honey over each slice and sprinkle with cinnamon.
4. Serve immediately.

Nutritional Information:
Kcal: 300 | Carb: 40g | Pro: 10g | Fat: 10g | Fib: 4g | Sod: 200mg

HERBED FRITTATA WITH COURGETTES AND PARMESAN

Prep Time: 5 minutes
Cook Time: 10 minutes
Difficulty: 3/10
Category: Gluten-Free, Vegetarian

Ingredients:

- 4 large eggs
- 1 small courgette, thinly sliced
- 30g Parmesan cheese, grated
- 1 tbsp fresh parsley, chopped
- 1 tbsp olive oil
- Salt and pepper, to taste

Instructions:

1. Preheat the grill to medium-high.
2. In a bowl, whisk together the eggs, Parmesan, parsley, salt, and pepper.
3. Heat the olive oil in a non-stick, oven-safe pan over medium heat.
4. Add the courgette slices and sauté for 2-3 minutes until slightly softened.
5. Pour the egg mixture over the courgettes and cook for 4-5 minutes until the edges begin to set.
6. Transfer the pan to the grill and cook for another 2-3 minutes until the top is golden and fully set.
7. Slice and serve.

Nutritional Information:
Kcal: 280 | Carb: 5g | Pro: 18g | Fat: 20g | Fib: 1g | Sod: 300mg150mg

CHIA PUDDING WITH ALMOND MILK AND FRESH FRUIT

Prep Time: 5 minutes
Cook Time: None (Chill Overnight)
Difficulty: 1/10
Category: Gluten-Free, Vegetarian, Vegan

Ingredients:

- 4 tbsp chia seeds
- 250ml almond milk (unsweetened)
- 1 tbsp maple syrup
- 100g mixed berries (strawberries, blueberries, raspberries)

Instructions:

1. In a bowl or jar, mix the chia seeds, almond milk, and maple syrup.
2. Stir well and let it sit for 5 minutes, then stir again to prevent clumping.
3. Cover and refrigerate overnight.
4. In the morning, top with mixed berries and serve.

Nutritional Information:
Kcal: 200 | Carb: 24g | Pro: 5g | Fat: 10g | Fib: 10g | Sod: 50mg

SPINACH AND MUSHROOM BREAKFAST QUESADILLA

Prep Time: 5 minutes
Cook Time: 10 minutes
Difficulty: 2/10
Category: Vegetarian

Ingredients:

- 2 large whole wheat tortillas
- 100g mushrooms, sliced
- 50g spinach, washed
- 50g grated cheddar cheese
- 1 tbsp olive oil
- Salt and pepper, to taste

Instructions:

1. Heat olive oil in a non-stick pan over medium heat.
2. Add the mushrooms and sauté for 3-4 minutes until browned.
3. Add the spinach and cook until wilted, about 1 minute. Season with salt and pepper.
4. Place one tortilla in the pan, sprinkle with half the cheese, and add the mushroom and spinach mixture.
5. Top with the remaining cheese and place the second tortilla on top.
6. Cook for 2-3 minutes on each side until the tortillas are golden and the cheese is melted.
7. Slice into wedges and serve.

Nutritional Information:
Kcal: 380 | Carb: 35g | Pro: 15g | Fat: 20g | Fib: 6g | Sod: 600mg20mg

LEMON AND POPPY SEED BREAKFAST LOAF

Prep Time: 10 minutes
Cook Time: 15 minutes
Difficulty: 3/10
Category: Vegetarian

Ingredients:

- 150g self-raising flour
- 100g caster sugar
- 2 large eggs
- 60ml extra virgin olive oil
- Zest and juice of 1 lemon
- 1 tbsp poppy seeds
- 1 tsp vanilla extract
- A pinch of salt

Instructions:

1. Preheat the oven to 180°C (160°C fan) and line a loaf tin with parchment paper.
2. In a large bowl, whisk together the eggs, sugar, olive oil, lemon zest, lemon juice, and vanilla extract.
3. Sift the flour, poppy seeds, and salt into the wet ingredients, and fold until just combined.
4. Pour the batter into the prepared loaf tin.
5. Bake for 15 minutes, or until a skewer inserted into the centre comes out clean.
6. Let cool before slicing and serving.

Nutritional Information:
Kcal: 200 | Carb: 28g | Pro: 4g | Fat: 8g | Fib: 1g | Sod: 60mg

FIG AND WALNUT BREAKFAST BARS

Prep Time: 10 minutes
Cook Time: 10 minutes
Difficulty: 3/10
Category: Vegetarian

Ingredients:

- 150g rolled oats
- 100g dried figs, chopped
- 50g walnuts, chopped
- 2 tbsp honey
- 2 tbsp almond butter
- 1 tsp vanilla extract
- A pinch of salt

Instructions:

1. Preheat the oven to 180°C (160°C fan) and line a baking tray with parchment paper.
2. In a large bowl, combine the oats, figs, and walnuts.
3. In a small saucepan, gently heat the honey and almond butter until smooth and well combined.
4. Stir in the vanilla extract and salt.
5. Pour the wet mixture over the dry ingredients and mix well.
6. Press the mixture into the prepared baking tray and bake for 10 minutes until golden.
7. Let cool before cutting into bars.

Nutritional Information:
Kcal: 250 | Carb: 35g | Pro: 5g | Fat: 10g | Fib: 4g | Sod: 50mg

GRILLED HALLOUMI AND TOMATO SANDWICH

Prep Time: 5 minutes
Cook Time: 10 minutes
Difficulty: 2/10
Category: Vegetarian

Ingredients:

- 4 slices whole grain bread
- 100g halloumi cheese, sliced
- 1 large tomato, sliced
- 1 tbsp olive oil
- Fresh basil leaves
- Salt and pepper, to taste

Instructions:

1. Heat a grill pan over medium heat and brush with olive oil.
2. Grill the halloumi slices for 2-3 minutes on each side until golden.
3. Toast the bread slices on the grill until slightly crisp.
4. Assemble the sandwich by layering the grilled halloumi, tomato slices, and fresh basil leaves between two slices of bread.
5. Season with salt and pepper, slice in half, and serve.

Nutritional Information:
Kcal: 400 | Carb: 40g | Pro: 20g | Fat: 20g | Fib: 6g | Sod: 700mg

MEDITERRANEAN BREAKFAST BOWL WITH QUINOA AND HUMMUS

Prep Time: 5 minutes
Cook Time: 10 minutes
Difficulty: 2/10
Category: Gluten-Free, Vegetarian, Vegan

Ingredients:

- 100g quinoa, rinsed
- 200ml water
- 2 tbsp hummus
- 100g cherry tomatoes, halved
- 1 small cucumber, diced
- 1 tbsp olive oil
- Fresh parsley for garnish
- Salt and pepper, to taste

Instructions:

1. In a medium saucepan, bring the quinoa and water to a boil. Reduce heat, cover, and simmer for 10 minutes until the quinoa is cooked and water is absorbed.
2. Divide the quinoa between two bowls.
3. Top each bowl with 1 tablespoon of hummus, cherry tomatoes, and cucumber.
4. Drizzle with olive oil and garnish with fresh parsley.
5. Season with salt and pepper, and serve.

Nutritional Information:
Kcal: 320 | Carb: 45g | Pro: 10g | Fat: 10g |
Fib: 6g | Sod: 250mg

SMOKED SALMON AND AVOCADO ON RYE BREAD

Prep Time: 5 minutes
Cook Time: None
Difficulty: 1/10
Category: Gluten-Free (if using gluten-free bread)

Ingredients:

- 2 slices rye bread (or gluten-free bread)
- 1 ripe avocado
- 100g smoked salmon
- 1 tbsp lemon juice
- Fresh dill for garnish
- Salt and pepper, to taste

Instructions:

1. Toast the slices of rye bread.
2. Mash the avocado in a small bowl with lemon juice, salt, and pepper.
3. Spread the mashed avocado evenly over the toast.
4. Top with smoked salmon and garnish with fresh dill.
5. Serve immediately.

Nutritional Information:
Kcal: 350 | Carb: 25g | Pro: 20g | Fat: 20g |
Fib: 8g | Sod: 600mg

EGG AND VEGETABLE BREAKFAST MUFFINS

Prep Time: 5 minutes
Cook Time: 15 minutes
Difficulty: 3/10
Category: Gluten-Free, Vegetarian

Ingredients:

- 4 large eggs
- 50g spinach, chopped
- 50g cherry tomatoes, halved
- 50g feta cheese, crumbled
- 1 tbsp olive oil
- Salt and pepper, to taste

Instructions:

1. Preheat the oven to 180°C (160°C fan) and grease a muffin tin with olive oil.
2. In a bowl, whisk the eggs with salt and pepper.
3. Stir in the spinach, cherry tomatoes, and feta cheese.
4. Pour the egg mixture evenly into the muffin tin.
5. Bake for 15 minutes, or until the muffins are set and golden.
6. Let cool slightly before serving.

Nutritional Information:
Kcal: 180 | Carb: 3g | Pro: 12g | Fat: 14g | Fib: 1g | Sod: 400mg

RICOTTA PANCAKES WITH BERRIES

Prep Time: 5 minutes
Cook Time: 10 minutes
Difficulty: 3/10
Category: Vegetarian

Ingredients:

- 150g ricotta cheese
- 2 large eggs
- 50g self-raising flour
- 1 tbsp sugar
- 1 tsp vanilla extract
- 100g mixed berries (strawberries, blueberries, raspberries)
- 1 tbsp olive oil for cooking

Instructions:

1. In a medium bowl, whisk together the ricotta cheese, eggs, sugar, and vanilla extract.
2. Sift in the flour and fold until just combined.
3. Heat a non-stick pan over medium heat and add a little olive oil.
4. Pour 2-3 tablespoons of batter per pancake into the pan, cooking for 2-3 minutes on each side until golden.
5. Serve the pancakes topped with fresh berries.

Nutritional Information:
Kcal: 320 | Carb: 35g | Pro: 14g | Fat: 14g | Fib: 3g | Sod: 120mg

SOUP AND SALADS

GREEK LENTIL SOUP (FAKES)

Prep Time: 5 minutes
Cook Time: 15 minutes
Difficulty: 3/10
Category: Gluten-Free, Vegetarian, Vegan

Ingredients:

- 100g brown lentils, rinsed
- 1 small onion, finely chopped
- 1 carrot, diced
- 1 celery stalk, diced
- 2 garlic cloves, minced
- 400ml vegetable broth
- 1 bay leaf
- 2 tbsp olive oil
- 1 tbsp red wine vinegar
- Salt and pepper, to taste

Instructions:

1. In a large pot, heat the olive oil over medium heat. Add the onion, carrot, and celery, and sauté for 3-4 minutes until softened.
2. Add the garlic and cook for another minute.
3. Stir in the lentils, vegetable broth, and bay leaf. Bring to a boil, then reduce heat and simmer for 15 minutes or until the lentils are tender.
4. Remove from heat, stir in the red wine vinegar, and season with salt and pepper.
5. Serve hot, with a drizzle of olive oil if desired.

Nutritional Information:
Kcal: 250 | Carb: 30g | Pro: 10g | Fat: 10g | Fib: 8g | Sod: 400mg150mg

MINESTRONE SOUP WITH SEASONAL VEGETABLES

Prep Time: 5 minutes
Cook Time: 15 minutes
Difficulty: 3/10
Category: Vegetarian

Ingredients:

- 1 small onion, chopped
- 1 carrot, diced
- 1 celery stalk, diced
- 1 courgette, diced
- 1 potato, diced
- 1 can (400g) chopped tomatoes
- 400ml vegetable broth
- 50g pasta (small shapes)
- 1 tbsp olive oil
- 1 tsp dried oregano
- Salt and pepper, to taste
- Fresh basil for garnish

Instructions:

1. Heat olive oil in a large pot over medium heat. Add the onion, carrot, and celery, and sauté for 3-4 minutes until softened.
2. Add the courgette and potato, and cook for another 2 minutes.
3. Stir in the chopped tomatoes, vegetable broth, and oregano. Bring to a boil, then reduce heat and simmer for 10 minutes.
4. Add the pasta and cook for another 5 minutes, or until the pasta is al dente.
5. Season with salt and pepper, and garnish with fresh basil before serving.

Nutritional Information:
Kcal: 300 | Carb: 50g | Pro: 8g | Fat: 8g | Fib: 10g | Sod: 600mg

TOMATO AND BASIL SOUP WITH OLIVE OIL

Prep Time: 5 minutes
Cook Time: 10 minutes
Difficulty: 2/10
Category: Gluten-Free, Vegetarian, Vegan

Ingredients:

- 1 can (400g) chopped tomatoes
- 1 small onion, chopped
- 2 garlic cloves, minced
- 400ml vegetable broth
- 1 tbsp olive oil
- 1 tsp sugar (optional)
- Salt and pepper, to taste
- Fresh basil leaves for garnish

Instructions:

1. Heat olive oil in a large pot over medium heat. Add the onion and sauté for 3-4 minutes until softened.
2. Add the garlic and cook for another minute.
3. Stir in the chopped tomatoes, vegetable broth, and sugar if using. Bring to a boil, then reduce heat and simmer for 10 minutes.
4. Season with salt and pepper to taste.
5. Serve hot, garnished with fresh basil leaves and a drizzle of olive oil.

Nutritional Information:
Kcal: 200 | Carb: 25g | Pro: 4g | Fat: 10g | Fib: 4g | Sod: 600mgg

ROASTED RED PEPPER AND TOMATO SOUP

Prep Time: 5 minutes
Cook Time: 10 minutes
Difficulty: 2/10
Category: Gluten-Free, Vegetarian, Vegan

Ingredients:

- 2 roasted red peppers, jarred or homemade
- 1 can (400g) chopped tomatoes
- 1 small onion, chopped
- 2 garlic cloves, minced
- 400ml vegetable broth
- 1 tbsp olive oil
- 1 tsp smoked paprika
- Salt and pepper, to taste

Instructions:

1. Heat olive oil in a large pot over medium heat. Add the onion and sauté for 3-4 minutes until softened.
2. Add the garlic and cook for another minute.
3. Stir in the chopped tomatoes, roasted red peppers, vegetable broth, and smoked paprika. Bring to a boil, then reduce heat and simmer for 10 minutes.
4. Use an immersion blender to blend the soup until smooth.
5. Season with salt and pepper, and serve hot.

Nutritional Information:
Kcal: 180 | Carb: 25g | Pro: 4g | Fat: 8g | Fib: 5g | Sod: 600mg

CHICKPEA AND SPINACH SOUP

Prep Time: 5 minutes
Cook Time: 10 minutes
Difficulty: 2/10
Category: Gluten-Free, Vegetarian, Vegan

Ingredients:

- 1 can (400g) chickpeas, drained and rinsed
- 100g spinach, washed
- 1 small onion, chopped
- 2 garlic cloves, minced
- 400ml vegetable broth
- 1 tbsp olive oil
- 1 tsp ground cumin
- Salt and pepper, to taste

Instructions:

1. Heat olive oil in a large pot over medium heat. Add the onion and sauté for 3-4 minutes until softened.
2. Add the garlic and cook for another minute.
3. Stir in the chickpeas, vegetable broth, and ground cumin. Bring to a boil, then reduce heat and simmer for 5 minutes.
4. Add the spinach and cook until wilted, about 2 minutes.
5. Season with salt and pepper, and serve hot.

Nutritional Information:
Kcal: 240 | Carb: 30g | Pro: 10g | Fat: 10g | Fib: 8g | Sod: 400mg

GREEK SALAD WITH FETA AND OLIVES

Prep Time: 5 minutes
Cook Time: None
Difficulty: 1/10
Category: Gluten-Free, Vegetarian

Ingredients:

- 2 large tomatoes, chopped
- 1 cucumber, sliced
- 1 small red onion, thinly sliced
- 100g feta cheese, crumbled
- 10 Kalamata olives, pitted
- 2 tbsp olive oil
- 1 tbsp red wine vinegar
- 1 tsp dried oregano
- Salt and pepper, to taste

Instructions:

1. In a large bowl, combine the tomatoes, cucumber, red onion, feta cheese, and olives.
2. Drizzle with olive oil and red wine vinegar.
3. Sprinkle with dried oregano, salt, and pepper.
4. Toss gently to combine and serve immediately.

Nutritional Information:
Kcal: 300 | Carb: 12g | Pro: 10g | Fat: 24g | Fib: 4g | Sod: 600mg

MEDITERRANEAN QUINOA SALAD WITH CUCUMBER AND MINT

Prep Time: 5 minutes
Cook Time: 10 minutes
Difficulty: 2/10
Category: Gluten-Free, Vegetarian, Vegan

Ingredients:

- 100g quinoa, rinsed
- 200ml water
- 1 cucumber, diced
- 10 cherry tomatoes, halved
- 2 tbsp fresh mint, chopped
- 2 tbsp olive oil
- 1 tbsp lemon juice
- Salt and pepper, to taste

Instructions:

1. In a medium saucepan, bring the quinoa and water to a boil. Reduce heat, cover, and simmer for 10 minutes until the quinoa is cooked and water is absorbed.
2. Let the quinoa cool slightly, then transfer to a large bowl.
3. Add the cucumber, cherry tomatoes, and fresh mint.
4. Drizzle with olive oil and lemon juice, and season with salt and pepper.
5. Toss gently to combine and serve.

Nutritional Information:
Kcal: 260 | Carb: 30g | Pro: 8g | Fat: 12g | Fib: 6g | Sod: 250mg

LENTIL AND BEETROOT SALAD WITH FETA

Prep Time: 5 minutes
Cook Time: 10 minutes
Difficulty: 2/10
Category: Gluten-Free, Vegetarian

Ingredients:

- 100g cooked lentils
- 2 medium beetroots, cooked and diced
- 50g feta cheese, crumbled
- 2 tbsp fresh parsley, chopped
- 2 tbsp olive oil
- 1 tbsp balsamic vinegar
- Salt and pepper, to taste

Instructions:

1. In a large bowl, combine the cooked lentils and diced beetroot.
2. Add the crumbled feta cheese and fresh parsley.
3. Drizzle with olive oil and balsamic vinegar.
4. Season with salt and pepper, and toss gently to combine.
5. Serve immediately.

Nutritional Information:
Kcal: 280 | Carb: 30g | Pro: 10g | Fat: 12g | Fib: 8g | Sod: 400mg

GRILLED VEGETABLE SALAD WITH BALSAMIC GLAZE

Prep Time: 5 minutes
Cook Time: 10 minutes
Difficulty: 3/10
Category: Gluten-Free, Vegetarian, Vegan

Ingredients:

- 1 red pepper, sliced
- 1 courgette, sliced
- 1 aubergine, sliced
- 1 red onion, sliced
- 2 tbsp olive oil
- 1 tbsp balsamic glaze
- Salt and pepper, to taste

Instructions:

1. Preheat a grill pan over medium heat.
2. Toss the sliced vegetables with olive oil, salt, and pepper.
3. Grill the vegetables for 3-4 minutes on each side until charred and tender.
4. Transfer the grilled vegetables to a serving platter.
5. Drizzle with balsamic glaze and serve.

Nutritional Information:
Kcal: 220 | Carb: 20g | Pro: 4g | Fat: 14g | Fib: 6g | Sod: 40mg

MEDITERRANEAN ORZO SALAD WITH SUN-DRIED TOMATOES

Prep Time: 5 minutes
Cook Time: 10 minutes
Difficulty: 2/10
Category: Vegetarian

Ingredients:

- 100g orzo pasta
- 50g sun-dried tomatoes, chopped
- 1 small red onion, finely chopped
- 10 Kalamata olives, pitted and halved
- 2 tbsp olive oil
- 1 tbsp lemon juice
- 1 tsp dried oregano
- Salt and pepper, to taste

Instructions:

1. Cook the orzo pasta according to package instructions. Drain and let cool slightly.
2. In a large bowl, combine the cooked orzo, sun-dried tomatoes, red onion, and olives.
3. Drizzle with olive oil and lemon juice, and sprinkle with dried oregano.
4. Season with salt and pepper, and toss gently to combine.
5. Serve immediately.

Nutritional Information:
Kcal: 300 | Carb: 45g | Pro: 8g | Fat: 10g | Fib: 4g | Sod: 600mgg

CHILLED CUCUMBER AND YOGURT SOUP (TZATZIKI SOUP)

Prep Time: 5 minutes
Cook Time: None (Chill for 10 minutes)
Difficulty: 1/10
Category: Gluten-Free, Vegetarian

Ingredients:

- 1 cucumber, peeled and chopped
- 300g Greek yogurt
- 1 garlic clove, minced
- 1 tbsp olive oil
- 1 tbsp fresh dill, chopped
- 1 tbsp lemon juice
- Salt and pepper, to taste

Instructions:

1. In a blender, combine the cucumber, Greek yogurt, garlic, olive oil, dill, and lemon juice.
2. Blend until smooth.
3. Season with salt and pepper.
4. Chill in the refrigerator for 10 minutes before serving.

Nutritional Information:
Kcal: 180 | Carb: 10g | Pro: 8g | Fat: 12g | Fib: 2g | Sod: 120mg

WARM FARRO AND ROASTED VEGETABLE SALAD

Prep Time: 5 minutes
Cook Time: 15 minutes
Difficulty: 3/10
Category: Vegetarian

Ingredients:

- 100g farro
- 1 small aubergine, diced
- 1 red pepper, diced
- 1 courgette, diced
- 2 tbsp olive oil
- 1 tbsp balsamic vinegar
- Salt and pepper, to taste
- Fresh basil for garnish

Instructions:

1. Preheat the oven to 200°C (180°C fan).
2. Toss the diced aubergine, red pepper, and courgette with 1 tablespoon of olive oil, salt, and pepper.
3. Spread the vegetables on a baking tray and roast for 15 minutes, or until tender and slightly charred.
4. While the vegetables are roasting, cook the farro according to package instructions. Drain and transfer to a large bowl.
5. Add the roasted vegetables to the farro.
6. Drizzle with the remaining olive oil and balsamic vinegar, and toss to combine.
7. Garnish with fresh basil and serve warm.

Nutritional Information:
Kcal: 320 | Carb: 45g | Pro: 10g | Fat: 12g | Fib: 8g | Sod: 40mg

CAULIFLOWER AND BROCCOLI SOUP

Prep Time: 5 minutes
Cook Time: 10 minutes
Difficulty: 2/10
Category: Gluten-Free, Vegetarian, Vegan

Ingredients:

- 1/2 head cauliflower, chopped
- 1/2 head broccoli, chopped
- 1 small onion, chopped
- 2 garlic cloves, minced
- 400ml vegetable broth
- 1 tbsp olive oil
- Salt and pepper, to taste

Instructions:

1. Heat olive oil in a large pot over medium heat. Add the onion and sauté for 3-4 minutes until softened.
2. Add the garlic and cook for another minute.
3. Stir in the cauliflower, broccoli, and vegetable broth. Bring to a boil, then reduce heat and simmer for 10 minutes until the vegetables are tender.
4. Use an immersion blender to blend the soup until smooth.
5. Season with salt and pepper, and serve hot.

Nutritional Information:
Kcal: 180 | Carb: 18g | Pro: 4g | Fat: 10g | Fib: 6g | Sod: 400mg

GREEK CHICKPEA SALAD WITH LEMON VINAIGRETTE

Prep Time: 5 minutes
Cook Time: None
Difficulty: 1/10
Category: Gluten-Free, Vegetarian, Vegan

Ingredients:

- 1 can (400g) chickpeas, drained and rinsed
- 1 cucumber, diced
- 10 cherry tomatoes, halved
- 10 Kalamata olives, pitted
- 2 tbsp olive oil
- 1 tbsp lemon juice
- 1 tsp dried oregano
- Salt and pepper, to taste

Instructions:

1. In a large bowl, combine the chickpeas, cucumber, cherry tomatoes, and olives.
2. Drizzle with olive oil and lemon juice.
3. Sprinkle with dried oregano, salt, and pepper.
4. Toss gently to combine and serve immediately.

Nutritional Information:
Kcal: 260 | Carb: 30g | Pro: 10g | Fat: 12g | Fib: 8g | Sod: 400mg

TUSCAN WHITE BEAN AND KALE SOUP

Prep Time: 5 minutes
Cook Time: 10 minutes
Difficulty: 3/10
Category: Gluten-Free, Vegetarian, Vegan

Ingredients:

- 1 can (400g) cannellini beans, drained and rinsed
- 100g kale, chopped
- 1 small onion, chopped
- 2 garlic cloves, minced
- 400ml vegetable broth
- 1 tbsp olive oil
- 1 tsp dried thyme
- Salt and pepper, to taste

Instructions:

1. Heat olive oil in a large pot over medium heat. Add the onion and sauté for 3-4 minutes until softened.
2. Add the garlic and cook for another minute.
3. Stir in the cannellini beans, kale, vegetable broth, and dried thyme. Bring to a boil, then reduce heat and simmer for 10 minutes.
4. Season with salt and pepper, and serve hot.

Nutritional Information:
Kcal: 220 | Carb: 30g | Pro: 10g | Fat: 8g | Fib: 10g | Sod: 400mg

TABBOULEH WITH FRESH PARSLEY AND MINT

Prep Time: 5 minutes
Cook Time: 10 minutes
Difficulty: 2/10
Category: Vegetarian, Vegan

Ingredients:

- 100g bulgur wheat
- 200ml water
- 2 large tomatoes, diced
- 1 cucumber, diced
- 1 small red onion, finely chopped
- 2 tbsp fresh parsley, chopped
- 2 tbsp fresh mint, chopped
- 2 tbsp olive oil
- 1 tbsp lemon juice
- Salt and pepper, to taste

Instructions:

1. In a medium saucepan, bring the bulgur wheat and water to a boil. Remove from heat, cover, and let it sit for 10 minutes until the bulgur is tender and the water is absorbed.
2. Let the bulgur cool slightly, then transfer to a large bowl.
3. Add the diced tomatoes, cucumber, red onion, parsley, and mint.
4. Drizzle with olive oil and lemon juice, and season with salt and pepper.
5. Toss gently to combine and serve.

Nutritional Information:
Kcal: 250 | Carb: 40g | Pro: 6g | Fat: 10g | Fib: 8g | Sod: 40mg

ROASTED BUTTERNUT SQUASH AND LENTIL SALAD

Prep Time: 5 minutes
Cook Time: 15 minutes
Difficulty: 3/10
Category: Gluten-Free, Vegetarian, Vegan

Ingredients:

- 200g butternut squash, peeled and diced
- 100g cooked lentils
- 2 tbsp olive oil
- 1 tbsp balsamic vinegar
- 1 tbsp fresh parsley, chopped
- Salt and pepper, to taste

Instructions:

1. Preheat the oven to 200°C (180°C fan).
2. Toss the diced butternut squash with 1 tablespoon of olive oil, salt, and pepper.
3. Spread the squash on a baking tray and roast for 15 minutes, or until tender and caramelized.
4. In a large bowl, combine the roasted butternut squash and cooked lentils.
5. Drizzle with the remaining olive oil and balsamic vinegar, and toss gently to combine.
6. Garnish with fresh parsley and serve warm.

Nutritional Information:
Kcal: 260 | Carb: 35g | Pro: 8g | Fat: 10g | Fib: 8g | Sod: 40mg

SPICY CARROT AND CORIANDER SOUP

Prep Time: 5 minutes
Cook Time: 10 minutes
Difficulty: 2/10
Category: Gluten-Free, Vegetarian, Vegan

Ingredients:

- 300g carrots, peeled and chopped
- 1 small onion, chopped
- 2 garlic cloves, minced
- 400ml vegetable broth
- 1 tbsp olive oil
- 1 tsp ground cumin
- 1 tsp ground coriander
- 1 tbsp fresh coriander, chopped
- Salt and pepper, to taste

Instructions:

1. Heat olive oil in a large pot over medium heat. Add the onion and sauté for 3-4 minutes until softened.
2. Add the garlic, cumin, and ground coriander, and cook for another minute.
3. Stir in the chopped carrots and vegetable broth. Bring to a boil, then reduce heat and simmer for 10 minutes until the carrots are tender.
4. Use an immersion blender to blend the soup until smooth.
5. Season with salt and pepper, and garnish with fresh coriander before serving.

Nutritional Information:
Kcal: 180 | Carb: 30g | Pro: 4g | Fat: 8g | Fib: 8g | Sod: 400mg

WATERMELON AND FETA SALAD WITH FRESH MINT

Prep Time: 5 minutes
Cook Time: None
Difficulty: 1/10
Category: Gluten-Free, Vegetarian

Ingredients:

- 300g watermelon, diced
- 100g feta cheese, crumbled
- 2 tbsp fresh mint, chopped
- 1 tbsp olive oil
- 1 tbsp balsamic vinegar
- Salt and pepper, to taste

Instructions:

1. In a large bowl, combine the diced watermelon and crumbled feta cheese.
2. Add the fresh mint.
3. Drizzle with olive oil and balsamic vinegar.
4. Season with salt and pepper, and toss gently to combine.
5. Serve immediately.

Nutritional Information:
Kcal: 220 | Carb: 25g | Pro: 8g | Fat: 12g | Fib: 2g | Sod: 300mg

CAPRESE SALAD WITH FRESH BASIL AND BALSAMIC REDUCTION

Prep Time: 5 minutes
Cook Time: None
Difficulty: 1/10
Category: Gluten-Free, Vegetarian

Ingredients:

- 2 large tomatoes, sliced
- 125g fresh mozzarella, sliced
- 10 fresh basil leaves
- 2 tbsp olive oil
- 1 tbsp balsamic reduction
- Salt and pepper, to taste

Instructions:

1. Arrange the tomato slices and mozzarella slices on a serving platter, alternating between the two.
2. Tuck the fresh basil leaves between the slices.
3. Drizzle with olive oil and balsamic reduction.
4. Season with salt and pepper, and serve immediately.

Nutritional Information:
Kcal: 250 | Carb: 10g | Pro: 12g | Fat: 18g | Fib: 2g | Sod: 300mg

DIPS AND SAUCES

CLASSIC HUMMUS WITH EXTRA VIRGIN OLIVE OIL

Prep Time: 5 minutes
Cook Time: None
Difficulty: 2/10
Category: Gluten-Free, Vegetarian, Vegan

Ingredients:

- 1 can (400g) chickpeas, drained and rinsed
- 2 tbsp tahini
- 2 tbsp extra virgin olive oil
- 2 tbsp lemon juice
- 1 garlic clove, minced
- Salt and pepper, to taste
- Water, as needed

Instructions:

1. In a food processor, combine the chickpeas, tahini, olive oil, lemon juice, and garlic.
2. Blend until smooth, adding water a tablespoon at a time until the desired consistency is reached.
3. Season with salt and pepper.
4. Transfer to a serving bowl, drizzle with extra virgin olive oil, and serve.

Nutritional Information:
Kcal: 300 | Carb: 30g | Pro: 10g | Fat: 16g | Fib: 8g | Sod: 200mg

BABA GANOUSH (ROASTED AUBERGINE DIP)

Prep Time: 5 minutes
Cook Time: 10 minutes (for roasting aubergine)
Difficulty: 3/10
Category: Gluten-Free, Vegetarian, Vegan

Ingredients:

- 1 large aubergine
- 2 tbsp tahini
- 2 tbsp lemon juice
- 2 garlic cloves, minced
- 2 tbsp extra virgin olive oil
- Salt and pepper, to taste
- Fresh parsley for garnish

Instructions:

1. Preheat the oven to 200°C (180°C fan). Prick the aubergine with a fork and place it on a baking tray.
2. Roast the aubergine for 10 minutes, turning occasionally, until soft and charred.
3. Let the aubergine cool, then peel off the skin and scoop out the flesh.
4. In a food processor, combine the aubergine flesh, tahini, lemon juice, garlic, and olive oil.
5. Blend until smooth, and season with salt and pepper.
6. Transfer to a serving bowl, garnish with fresh parsley, and serve.

Nutritional Information:
Kcal: 200 | Carb: 15g | Pro: 3g | Fat: 14g | Fib: 6g | Sod: 100mg

TZATZIKI (CUCUMBER AND YOGURT DIP)

Prep Time: 5 minutes
Cook Time: None
Difficulty: 1/10
Category: Gluten-Free, Vegetarian

Ingredients:

- 1/2 cucumber, grated
- 200g Greek yogurt
- 1 garlic clove, minced
- 1 tbsp lemon juice
- 1 tbsp fresh dill, chopped
- 1 tbsp extra virgin olive oil
- Salt and pepper, to taste

Instructions:

1. Grate the cucumber and squeeze out any excess water using a clean towel.
2. In a bowl, combine the Greek yogurt, grated cucumber, garlic, lemon juice, dill, and olive oil.
3. Season with salt and pepper, and mix well.
4. Serve immediately or refrigerate until needed.

Nutritional Information:
Kcal: 120 | Carb: 6g | Pro: 6g | Fat: 8g | Fib: 1g | Sod: 60mg

MUHAMMARA (ROASTED RED PEPPER AND WALNUT DIP)

Prep Time: 5 minutes
Cook Time: 10 minutes (for roasting peppers)
Difficulty: 3/10
Category: Gluten-Free, Vegetarian, Vegan

Ingredients:

- 2 roasted red peppers, jarred or homemade
- 50g walnuts
- 2 tbsp breadcrumbs (use gluten-free if necessary)
- 2 tbsp extra virgin olive oil
- 1 tbsp lemon juice
- 1 garlic clove, minced
- 1 tsp ground cumin
- Salt and pepper, to taste

Instructions:

1. If roasting your own peppers, preheat the oven to 200°C (180°C fan), place the peppers on a baking tray, and roast for 10 minutes until charred.
2. In a food processor, combine the roasted red peppers, walnuts, breadcrumbs, olive oil, lemon juice, garlic, and ground cumin.
3. Blend until smooth, and season with salt and pepper.
4. Transfer to a serving bowl and serve.

Nutritional Information:
Kcal: 250 | Carb: 15g | Pro: 5g | Fat: 20g | Fib: 4g | Sod: 200mg

ROASTED GARLIC AND LEMON AIOLI

Prep Time: 5 minutes
Cook Time: 10 minutes (for roasting garlic)
Difficulty: 3/10
Category: Gluten-Free, Vegetarian

Ingredients:

- 1 whole garlic bulb
- 1 egg yolk
- 1 tbsp lemon juice
- 100ml olive oil
- Salt and pepper, to taste

Instructions:

1. Preheat the oven to 200°C (180°C fan). Cut the top off the garlic bulb to expose the cloves, drizzle with olive oil, wrap in foil, and roast for 10 minutes until soft.
2. Squeeze the roasted garlic cloves out of their skins and mash into a paste.
3. In a bowl, whisk together the egg yolk and lemon juice.
4. Slowly add the olive oil in a thin stream, whisking constantly until emulsified.
5. Stir in the mashed garlic and season with salt and pepper.
6. Serve immediately.

Nutritional Information:
Kcal: 220 | Carb: 3g | Pro: 2g | Fat: 22g | Fib: 1g | Sod: 40mg

SPICY HARISSA SAUCE

Prep Time: 5 minutes
Cook Time: None
Difficulty: 2/10
Category: Gluten-Free, Vegetarian, Vegan

Ingredients:

- 4 dried red chilies, soaked in warm water until soft
- 2 garlic cloves, minced
- 1 tsp ground cumin
- 1 tsp ground coriander
- 2 tbsp tomato paste
- 2 tbsp extra virgin olive oil
- 1 tbsp lemon juice
- Salt, to taste

Instructions:

1. In a food processor, combine the soaked chilies, garlic, ground cumin, ground coriander, tomato paste, olive oil, and lemon juice.
2. Blend until smooth, adding a little water if needed to reach the desired consistency.
3. Season with salt and adjust the spice level if necessary.
4. Serve immediately or refrigerate until needed.

Nutritional Information:
Kcal: 100 | Carb: 6g | Pro: 2g | Fat: 8g | Fib: 2g | Sod: 200mg

OLIVE TAPENADE WITH CAPERS AND ANCHOVIES

Prep Time: 5 minutes
Cook Time: None
Difficulty: 2/10
Category: Gluten-Free

Ingredients:

- 100g Kalamata olives, pitted
- 1 tbsp capers, rinsed
- 2 anchovy fillets
- 1 garlic clove, minced
- 2 tbsp extra virgin olive oil
- 1 tbsp lemon juice
- Black pepper, to taste

Instructions:

1. In a food processor, combine the olives, capers, anchovy fillets, garlic, olive oil, and lemon juice.
2. Blend until a coarse paste forms.
3. Season with black pepper and adjust the consistency with more olive oil if needed.
4. Serve immediately or refrigerate until needed.

Nutritional Information:
Kcal: 150 | Carb: 4g | Pro: 2g | Fat: 14g | Fib: 2g | Sod: 800mg

GREEK SKORDALIA (GARLIC AND POTATO DIP)

Prep Time: 5 minutes
Cook Time: 10 minutes (for boiling potatoes)
Difficulty: 3/10
Category: Gluten-Free, Vegetarian, Vegan

Ingredients:

- 200g potatoes, peeled and diced
- 3 garlic cloves, minced
- 2 tbsp extra virgin olive oil
- 2 tbsp lemon juice
- Salt and pepper, to taste

Instructions:

1. Boil the diced potatoes in salted water for 10 minutes, or until tender. Drain and let cool slightly.
2. In a food processor, combine the cooked potatoes, garlic, olive oil, and lemon juice.
3. Blend until smooth, adding a little water if needed to reach the desired consistency.
4. Season with salt and pepper.
5. Serve immediately or refrigerate until needed.

Nutritional Information:
Kcal: 180 | Carb: 24g | Pro: 3g | Fat: 8g | Fib: 3g | Sod: 200mg

SUN-DRIED TOMATO PESTO

Prep Time: 5 minutes
Cook Time: None
Difficulty: 2/10
Category: Gluten-Free, Vegetarian

Ingredients:

- 50g sun-dried tomatoes, drained
- 30g Parmesan cheese, grated
- 30g pine nuts
- 1 garlic clove, minced
- 2 tbsp extra virgin olive oil
- 1 tbsp lemon juice
- Salt and pepper, to taste

Instructions:

1. In a food processor, combine the sun-dried tomatoes, Parmesan cheese, pine nuts, garlic, olive oil, and lemon juice.
2. Blend until smooth, adding a little water if needed to reach the desired consistency.
3. Season with salt and pepper.
4. Serve immediately or refrigerate until needed.

Nutritional Information:
Kcal: 200 | Carb: 6g | Pro: 5g | Fat: 18g | Fib: 2g | Sod: 300mg

HERBED YOGURT SAUCE WITH DILL AND MINT

Prep Time: 5 minutes
Cook Time: None
Difficulty: 1/10
Category: Gluten-Free, Vegetarian

Ingredients:

- 200g Greek yogurt
- 1 tbsp fresh dill, chopped
- 1 tbsp fresh mint, chopped
- 1 garlic clove, minced
- 1 tbsp lemon juice
- Salt and pepper, to taste

Instructions:

1. In a bowl, combine the Greek yogurt, dill, mint, garlic, and lemon juice.
2. Season with salt and pepper, and mix well.
3. Serve immediately or refrigerate until needed.

Nutritional Information:
Kcal: 100 | Carb: 6g | Pro: 6g | Fat: 6g | Fib: 0g | Sod: 60mg

ROASTED RED PEPPER AND FETA DIP

Prep Time: 5 minutes
Cook Time: 10 minutes (for roasting peppers)
Difficulty: 3/10
Category: Gluten-Free, Vegetarian

Ingredients:

- 2 roasted red peppers, jarred or homemade
- 50g feta cheese, crumbled
- 1 garlic clove, minced
- 2 tbsp extra virgin olive oil
- 1 tbsp lemon juice
- Salt and pepper, to taste

Instructions:

1. If roasting your own peppers, preheat the oven to 200°C (180°C fan), place the peppers on a baking tray, and roast for 10 minutes until charred.
2. In a food processor, combine the roasted red peppers, feta cheese, garlic, olive oil, and lemon juice.
3. Blend until smooth, and season with salt and pepper.
4. Serve immediately or refrigerate until needed.

Nutritional Information:
Kcal: 220 | Carb: 8g | Pro: 6g | Fat: 18g | Fib: 2g | Sod: 400mg

LEMON AND HERB TAHINI SAUCE

Prep Time: 5 minutes
Cook Time: None
Difficulty: 1/10
Category: Gluten-Free, Vegetarian, Vegan

Ingredients:

- 2 tbsp tahini
- 2 tbsp lemon juice
- 2 tbsp water
- 1 garlic clove, minced
- 1 tbsp fresh parsley, chopped
- Salt and pepper, to taste

Instructions:

1. In a bowl, whisk together the tahini, lemon juice, and water until smooth.
2. Stir in the garlic and parsley.
3. Season with salt and pepper.
4. Serve immediately or refrigerate until needed.

Nutritional Information:
Kcal: 150 | Carb: 6g | Pro: 4g | Fat: 12g | Fib: 2g | Sod: 40mg

AVOCADO AND CILANTRO DIP

Prep Time: 5 minutes
Cook Time: None
Difficulty: 1/10
Category: Gluten-Free, Vegetarian, Vegan

Ingredients:

- 1 ripe avocado
- 1 tbsp fresh cilantro, chopped
- 1 garlic clove, minced
- 1 tbsp lime juice
- Salt and pepper, to taste

Instructions:

1. In a bowl, mash the avocado with a fork until smooth.
2. Stir in the cilantro, garlic, and lime juice.
3. Season with salt and pepper.
4. Serve immediately.

Nutritional Information:
Kcal: 160 | Carb: 8g | Pro: 2g | Fat: 14g | Fib: 6g | Sod: 20mg

GREEN OLIVE AND ALMOND TAPENADE

Prep Time: 5 minutes
Cook Time: None
Difficulty: 2/10
Category: Gluten-Free, Vegetarian, Vegan

Ingredients:

- 100g green olives, pitted
- 30g almonds
- 1 garlic clove, minced
- 2 tbsp extra virgin olive oil
- 1 tbsp lemon juice
- Salt and pepper, to taste

Instructions:

1. In a food processor, combine the green olives, almonds, garlic, olive oil, and lemon juice.
2. Blend until a coarse paste forms.
3. Season with salt and pepper.
4. Serve immediately or refrigerate until needed.

Nutritional Information:
Kcal: 180 | Carb: 4g | Pro: 3g | Fat: 18g | Fib: 3g | Sod: 400mg

SMOKED PAPRIKA AIOLI

Prep Time: 5 minutes
Cook Time: None
Difficulty: 2/10
Category: Gluten-Free, Vegetarian

Ingredients:

- 1 egg yolk
- 1 garlic clove, minced
- 1 tsp smoked paprika
- 100ml olive oil
- 1 tbsp lemon juice
- Salt, to taste

Instructions:

1. In a bowl, whisk together the egg yolk, garlic, and smoked paprika.
2. Slowly add the olive oil in a thin stream, whisking constantly until emulsified.
3. Stir in the lemon juice and season with salt.
4. Serve immediately.

Nutritional Information:
Kcal: 220 | Carb: 1g | Pro: 2g | Fat: 22g | Fib: 0g | Sod: 40mg

FRESH TOMATO AND BASIL SALSA

Prep Time: 5 minutes
Cook Time: None
Difficulty: 1/10
Category: Gluten-Free, Vegetarian, Vegan

Ingredients:

- 2 large tomatoes, diced
- 1 small red onion, finely chopped
- 1 garlic clove, minced
- 2 tbsp fresh basil, chopped
- 1 tbsp extra virgin olive oil
- Salt and pepper, to taste

Instructions:

1. In a bowl, combine the diced tomatoes, red onion, garlic, and basil.
2. Drizzle with olive oil and season with salt and pepper.
3. Toss gently to combine and serve immediately.

Nutritional Information:
Kcal: 80 | Carb: 10g | Pro: 2g | Fat: 4g | Fib: 2g | Sod: 20mg

GARLIC AND LEMON TAHINI DRESSING

Prep Time: 5 minutes
Cook Time: None
Difficulty: 1/10
Category: Gluten-Free, Vegetarian, Vegan

Ingredients:

- 2 tbsp tahini
- 2 tbsp lemon juice
- 1 garlic clove, minced
- 2 tbsp water
- Salt and pepper, to taste

Instructions:

1. In a bowl, whisk together the tahini, lemon juice, garlic, and water until smooth.
2. Season with salt and pepper.
3. Serve immediately or refrigerate until needed.

Nutritional Information:
Kcal: 150 | Carb: 6g | Pro: 4g | Fat: 12g | Fib: 2g | Sod: 40mg

CHIMICHURRI SAUCE WITH PARSLEY AND OREGANO

Prep Time: 5 minutes
Cook Time: None
Difficulty: 1/10
Category: Gluten-Free, Vegetarian, Vegan

Ingredients:

- 1/2 cup fresh parsley, chopped
- 2 tbsp fresh oregano, chopped
- 2 garlic cloves, minced
- 2 tbsp red wine vinegar
- 4 tbsp extra virgin olive oil
- Salt and pepper, to taste

Instructions:

1. In a bowl, combine the parsley, oregano, garlic, and red wine vinegar.
2. Slowly add the olive oil while stirring.
3. Season with salt and pepper.
4. Serve immediately or refrigerate until needed.

Nutritional Information:
Kcal: 200 | Carb: 1g | Pro: 1g | Fat: 22g | Fib: 1g | Sod: 20mg

PESTO GENOVESE WITH BASIL AND PINE NUTS

Prep Time: 5 minutes
Cook Time: None
Difficulty: 2/10
Category: Gluten-Free, Vegetarian

Ingredients:

- 1 cup fresh basil leaves
- 30g pine nuts
- 30g Parmesan cheese, grated
- 1 garlic clove, minced
- 4 tbsp extra virgin olive oil
- Salt and pepper, to taste

Instructions:

1. In a food processor, combine the basil leaves, pine nuts, Parmesan cheese, and garlic.
2. Blend while slowly adding the olive oil until smooth.
3. Season with salt and pepper.
4. Serve immediately or refrigerate until needed.

Nutritional Information:
Kcal: 250 | Carb: 4g | Pro: 5g | Fat: 24g | Fib: 2g | Sod: 200mg

LEMON-CAPER VINAIGRETTE

Prep Time: 5 minutes
Cook Time: None
Difficulty: 1/10
Category: Gluten-Free, Vegetarian, Vegan

Ingredients:

- 2 tbsp lemon juice
- 1 tbsp capers, rinsed and chopped
- 4 tbsp extra virgin olive oil
- 1 garlic clove, minced
- Salt and pepper, to taste

Instructions:

1. In a bowl, whisk together the lemon juice, capers, olive oil, and garlic.
2. Season with salt and pepper.
3. Serve immediately or refrigerate until needed.

Nutritional Information:
Kcal: 180 | Carb: 2g | Pro: 1g | Fat: 20g | Fib: 0g | Sod: 200mg

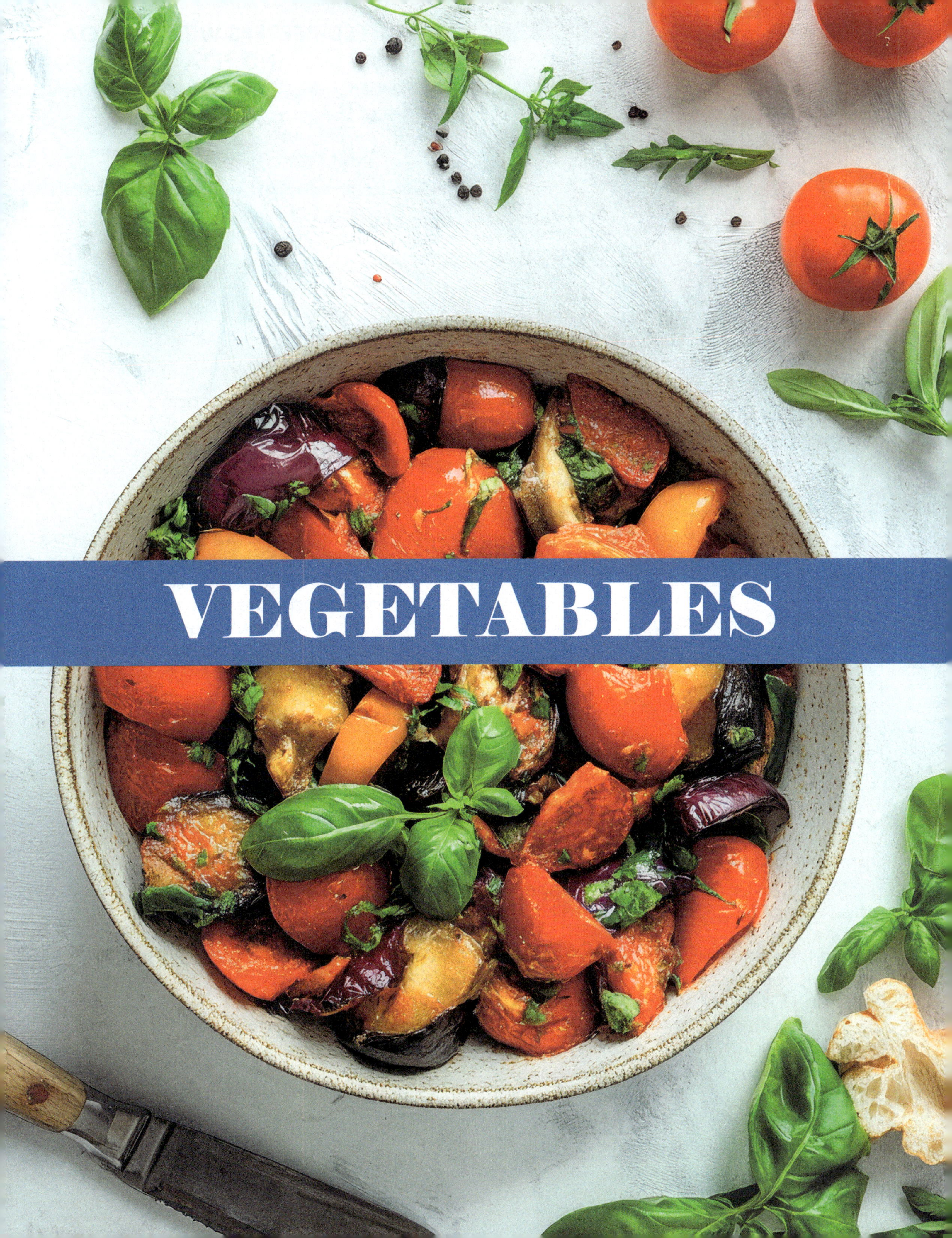

VEGETABLES

ROASTED MEDITERRANEAN VEGETABLES WITH THYME

Prep Time: 5 minutes
Cook Time: 15 minutes
Difficulty: 2/10
Category: Gluten-Free, Vegetarian, Vegan

Ingredients:

- 1 red pepper, chopped
- 1 yellow pepper, chopped
- 1 courgette, sliced
- 1 red onion, chopped
- 1 aubergine, diced
- 2 tbsp olive oil
- 1 tsp dried thyme
- Salt and pepper, to taste

Instructions:

1. Preheat the oven to 200°C (180°C fan).
2. In a large bowl, toss the chopped vegetables with olive oil, dried thyme, salt, and pepper.
3. Spread the vegetables on a baking tray in a single layer.
4. Roast for 15 minutes, stirring halfway through, until tender and slightly caramelised.
5. Serve immediately.

Nutritional Information:
Kcal: 200 | Carb: 20g | Pro: 4g | Fat: 12g | Fib: 6g | Sod: 60mg

STUFFED PEPPERS WITH QUINOA AND FETA

Prep Time: 10 minutes
Cook Time: 15 minutes
Difficulty: 3/10
Category: Gluten-Free, Vegetarian

Ingredients:

- 2 large bell peppers, halved and seeded
- 100g quinoa, rinsed
- 200ml water
- 50g feta cheese, crumbled
- 1 small red onion, chopped
- 1 tbsp olive oil
- 1 tbsp fresh parsley, chopped
- Salt and pepper, to taste

Instructions:

1. Preheat the oven to 200°C (180°C fan).
2. In a medium saucepan, bring the quinoa and water to a boil. Reduce heat, cover, and simmer for 10 minutes until the quinoa is cooked and water is absorbed.
3. In a large bowl, combine the cooked quinoa, feta cheese, red onion, olive oil, parsley, salt, and pepper.
4. Stuff the pepper halves with the quinoa mixture and place them on a baking tray.
5. Bake for 15 minutes, or until the peppers are tender.
6. Serve immediately.

Nutritional Information:
Kcal: 250 | Carb: 30g | Pro: 8g | Fat: 12g | Fib: 6g | Sod: 400mg

SAUTÉED SPINACH WITH GARLIC AND PINE NUTS

Prep Time: 5 minutes
Cook Time: 5 minutes
Difficulty: 2/10
Category: Gluten-Free, Vegetarian, Vegan

Ingredients:

- 200g fresh spinach, washed
- 2 garlic cloves, minced
- 2 tbsp pine nuts
- 1 tbsp olive oil
- Salt and pepper, to taste

Instructions:

1. Heat olive oil in a large pan over medium heat.
2. Add the garlic and sauté for 1 minute until fragrant.
3. Add the spinach and cook, stirring, until wilted, about 2-3 minutes.
4. Stir in the pine nuts and cook for an additional 1-2 minutes.
5. Season with salt and pepper, and serve immediately.

Nutritional Information:
Kcal: 180 | Carb: 6g | Pro: 4g | Fat: 16g | Fib: 4g | Sod: 100mg

RATATOUILLE WITH FRESH HERBS

Prep Time: 10 minutes
Cook Time: 15 minutes
Difficulty: 3/10
Category: Gluten-Free, Vegetarian, Vegan

Ingredients:

- 1 aubergine, diced
- 1 courgette, sliced
- 1 red pepper, chopped
- 1 onion, chopped
- 2 tomatoes, chopped
- 2 garlic cloves, minced
- 2 tbsp olive oil
- 1 tsp dried thyme
- 1 tsp dried basil
- Salt and pepper, to taste

Instructions:

1. Heat olive oil in a large pan over medium heat.
2. Add the onion and garlic, and sauté for 3-4 minutes until softened.
3. Add the aubergine, courgette, and red pepper, and cook for 5 minutes, stirring occasionally.
4. Stir in the tomatoes, dried thyme, and dried basil. Cook for another 5 minutes until the vegetables are tender.
5. Season with salt and pepper, and serve immediately.

Nutritional Information:
Kcal: 220 | Carb: 24g | Pro: 4g | Fat: 12g | Fib: 8g | Sod: 80mg

GRILLED AUBERGINE WITH TAHINI AND POMEGRANATE

Prep Time: 5 minutes
Cook Time: 10 minutes
Difficulty: 3/10
Category: Gluten-Free, Vegetarian, Vegan

Ingredients:

- 1 large aubergine, sliced lengthwise
- 2 tbsp tahini
- 1 tbsp lemon juice
- 2 tbsp pomegranate seeds
- 1 tbsp olive oil
- Salt and pepper, to taste
- Fresh parsley for garnish

Instructions:

1. Preheat a grill pan over medium heat and brush with olive oil.
2. Grill the aubergine slices for 3-4 minutes on each side until tender and charred.
3. In a small bowl, mix the tahini and lemon juice with a little water to thin if needed.
4. Arrange the grilled aubergine on a serving plate, drizzle with the tahini sauce, and sprinkle with pomegranate seeds.
5. Garnish with fresh parsley and serve immediately.

Nutritional Information:
Kcal: 200 | Carb: 15g | Pro: 4g | Fat: 14g | Fib: 6g | Sod: 60mg

ROASTED CAULIFLOWER WITH CUMIN AND CORIANDER

Prep Time: 5 minutes
Cook Time: 15 minutes
Difficulty: 2/10
Category: Gluten-Free, Vegetarian, Vegan

Ingredients:

- 1 small cauliflower, cut into florets
- 2 tbsp olive oil
- 1 tsp ground cumin
- 1 tsp ground coriander
- Salt and pepper, to taste

Instructions:

1. Preheat the oven to 200°C (180°C fan).
2. In a large bowl, toss the cauliflower florets with olive oil, cumin, coriander, salt, and pepper.
3. Spread the cauliflower on a baking tray in a single layer.
4. Roast for 15 minutes, or until tender and golden.
5. Serve immediately.

Nutritional Information:
Kcal: 150 | Carb: 12g | Pro: 3g | Fat: 10g | Fib: 4g | Sod: 80mg

BAKED TOMATOES STUFFED WITH RICE AND HERBS

Prep Time: 10 minutes
Cook Time: 15 minutes
Difficulty: 3/10
Category: Gluten-Free, Vegetarian, Vegan

Ingredients:

- 4 large tomatoes, tops cut off and insides scooped out
- 100g cooked rice
- 1 small onion, finely chopped
- 1 garlic clove, minced
- 1 tbsp fresh parsley, chopped
- 1 tbsp fresh mint, chopped
- 2 tbsp olive oil
- Salt and pepper, to taste

Instructions:

1. Preheat the oven to 200°C (180°C fan).
2. In a bowl, mix the cooked rice, onion, garlic, parsley, mint, olive oil, salt, and pepper.
3. Stuff each tomato with the rice mixture and place them in a baking dish.
4. Drizzle with a little olive oil and bake for 15 minutes, or until the tomatoes are tender.
5. Serve immediately.

Nutritional Information:
Kcal: 220 | Carb: 30g | Pro: 4g | Fat: 10g | Fib: 4g | Sod: 100mg

COURGETTE FRITTERS WITH TZATZIKI

Prep Time: 10 minutes
Cook Time: 5 minutes
Difficulty: 3/10
Category: Gluten-Free, Vegetarian

Ingredients:

- 2 medium courgettes, grated
- 1 egg, beaten
- 50g gluten-free flour
- 2 tbsp fresh dill, chopped
- 2 tbsp olive oil
- Salt and pepper, to taste
- For the Tzatziki:
- 100g Greek yogurt
- 1/2 cucumber, grated and drained
- 1 garlic clove, minced
- 1 tbsp lemon juice
- Salt, to taste

Instructions:

1. Grate the courgettes and squeeze out any excess moisture using a clean towel.
2. In a bowl, combine the grated courgettes, beaten egg, flour, dill, salt, and pepper.
3. Heat olive oil in a non-stick pan over medium heat.
4. Drop spoonfuls of the mixture into the pan and flatten slightly. Cook for 2-3 minutes on each side until golden brown.
5. In a small bowl, mix all the ingredients for the tzatziki.
6. Serve the fritters hot with tzatziki on the side.

Nutritional Information:
Kcal: 250 | Carb: 24g | Pro: 8g | Fat: 14g | Fib: 4g | Sod: 200mg

BRAISED GREEN BEANS WITH TOMATOES AND ONIONS

Prep Time: 5 minutes
Cook Time: 10 minutes
Difficulty: 2/10
Category: Gluten-Free, Vegetarian, Vegan

Ingredients:

- 200g green beans, trimmed
- 1 small onion, sliced
- 2 garlic cloves, minced
- 2 tomatoes, chopped
- 2 tbsp olive oil
- Salt and pepper, to taste

Instructions:

1. Heat olive oil in a large pan over medium heat.
2. Add the sliced onion and sauté for 3-4 minutes until softened.
3. Add the garlic and cook for another minute.
4. Stir in the chopped tomatoes and cook for 2 minutes.
5. Add the green beans and a splash of water. Cover and cook for 5 minutes until the beans are tender.
6. Season with salt and pepper, and serve immediately.

Nutritional Information:
Kcal: 160 | Carb: 12g | Pro: 4g | Fat: 12g | Fib: 4g | Sod: 80mg

CRISPY OVEN-ROASTED POTATOES WITH ROSEMARY

Prep Time: 5 minutes
Cook Time: 15 minutes
Difficulty: 2/10
Category: Gluten-Free, Vegetarian, Vegan

Ingredients:

- 400g baby potatoes, halved
- 2 tbsp olive oil
- 1 tsp dried rosemary
- Salt and pepper, to taste

Instructions:

1. Preheat the oven to 200°C (180°C fan).
2. In a large bowl, toss the halved potatoes with olive oil, rosemary, salt, and pepper.
3. Spread the potatoes on a baking tray in a single layer.
4. Roast for 15 minutes, or until golden and crispy, stirring halfway through.
5. Serve immediately.

Nutritional Information:
Kcal: 220 | Carb: 36g | Pro: 4g | Fat: 8g | Fib: 4g | Sod: 40mg

SAUTÉED MUSHROOMS WITH GARLIC AND PARSLEY

Prep Time: 5 minutes
Cook Time: 10 minutes
Difficulty: 2/10
Category: Gluten-Free, Vegetarian, Vegan

Ingredients:

- 200g mushrooms, sliced
- 2 garlic cloves, minced
- 2 tbsp olive oil
- 1 tbsp fresh parsley, chopped
- Salt and pepper, to taste

Instructions:

1. Heat olive oil in a large pan over medium heat.
2. Add the garlic and sauté for 1 minute until fragrant.
3. Add the sliced mushrooms and cook for 5-7 minutes until golden and soft.
4. Stir in the chopped parsley and season with salt and pepper.
5. Serve immediately.

Nutritional Information:
Kcal: 160 | Carb: 6g | Pro: 4g | Fat: 14g | Fib: 2g | Sod: 60mg

CARAMELISED ONIONS AND PEPPERS

Prep Time: 5 minutes
Cook Time: 10 minutes
Difficulty: 2/10
Category: Gluten-Free, Vegetarian, Vegan

Ingredients:

- 2 large onions, thinly sliced
- 1 red pepper, thinly sliced
- 1 yellow pepper, thinly sliced
- 2 tbsp olive oil
- 1 tsp balsamic vinegar
- Salt and pepper, to taste

Instructions:

1. Heat olive oil in a large pan over medium heat.
2. Add the sliced onions and peppers, and cook for 8-10 minutes, stirring occasionally, until soft and caramelised.
3. Stir in the balsamic vinegar and cook for an additional minute.
4. Season with salt and pepper, and serve immediately.

Nutritional Information:
Kcal: 180 | Carb: 20g | Pro: 2g | Fat: 10g | Fib: 4g | Sod: 40mg

GRILLED ASPARAGUS WITH LEMON AND OLIVE OIL

Prep Time: 5 minutes
Cook Time: 10 minutes
Difficulty: 2/10
Category: Gluten-Free, Vegetarian, Vegan

Ingredients:

- 200g asparagus, trimmed
- 2 tbsp olive oil
- 1 tbsp lemon juice
- Salt and pepper, to taste

Instructions:

1. Preheat a grill pan over medium heat and brush with olive oil.
2. Grill the asparagus for 5-7 minutes, turning occasionally, until tender and slightly charred.
3. Transfer to a serving plate, drizzle with lemon juice, and season with salt and pepper.
4. Serve immediately.

Nutritional Information:
Kcal: 120 | Carb: 6g | Pro: 3g | Fat: 10g | Fib: 2g | Sod: 40mg

MARINATED ARTICHOKE HEARTS

Prep Time: 5 minutes
Cook Time: None (Marinate for 10 minutes)
Difficulty: 1/10
Category: Gluten-Free, Vegetarian, Vegan

Ingredients:

- 200g artichoke hearts, drained and quartered
- 2 tbsp extra virgin olive oil
- 1 tbsp lemon juice
- 1 garlic clove, minced
- 1 tsp dried oregano
- Salt and pepper, to taste

Instructions:

1. In a bowl, combine the artichoke hearts, olive oil, lemon juice, garlic, and oregano.
2. Season with salt and pepper, and toss to coat.
3. Let the artichokes marinate for at least 10 minutes before serving.
4. Serve chilled or at room temperature.

Nutritional Information:
Kcal: 180 | Carb: 10g | Pro: 4g | Fat: 14g | Fib: 6g | Sod: 100mg

SPINACH AND RICOTTA STUFFED AUBERGINES

Prep Time: 10 minutes
Cook Time: 15 minutes
Difficulty: 3/10
Category: Gluten-Free, Vegetarian

Ingredients:

- 1 large aubergine, halved lengthwise
- 100g spinach, washed
- 100g ricotta cheese
- 1 garlic clove, minced
- 2 tbsp Parmesan cheese, grated
- 2 tbsp olive oil
- Salt and pepper, to taste

Instructions:

1. Preheat the oven to 200°C (180°C fan).
2. Scoop out the flesh of the aubergine halves, leaving a 1cm thick shell. Chop the scooped-out flesh and set aside.
3. Heat olive oil in a pan over medium heat. Add the garlic and sauté for 1 minute.
4. Add the chopped aubergine flesh and spinach, and cook for 5 minutes until softened.
5. Stir in the ricotta cheese and season with salt and pepper.
6. Stuff the aubergine shells with the spinach and ricotta mixture, top with grated Parmesan, and place on a baking tray.
7. Bake for 15 minutes, or until the aubergines are tender and the cheese is golden.
8. Serve immediately.

Nutritional Information:
Kcal: 320 | Carb: 12g | Pro: 10g | Fat: 26g | Fib: 6g | Sod: 300mg

HERBED ROASTED CARROTS

Prep Time: 5 minutes
Cook Time: 15 minutes
Difficulty: 2/10
Category: Gluten-Free, Vegetarian, Vegan

Ingredients:

- 300g carrots, peeled and sliced lengthwise
- 2 tbsp olive oil
- 1 tsp dried thyme
- 1 tsp dried rosemary
- Salt and pepper, to taste

Instructions:

1. Preheat the oven to 200°C (180°C fan).
2. In a large bowl, toss the carrots with olive oil, thyme, rosemary, salt, and pepper.
3. Spread the carrots on a baking tray in a single layer.
4. Roast for 15 minutes, or until tender and slightly caramelised.
5. Serve immediately.

Nutritional Information:
Kcal: 160 | Carb: 18g | Pro: 2g | Fat: 10g | Fib: 6g | Sod: 40mg

GREEK-STYLE ROASTED POTATOES WITH LEMON AND OREGANO

Prep Time: 5 minutes
Cook Time: 15 minutes
Difficulty: 2/10
Category: Gluten-Free, Vegetarian, Vegan

Ingredients:

- 400g baby potatoes, halved
- 2 tbsp olive oil
- 1 tbsp lemon juice
- 1 tsp dried oregano
- Salt and pepper, to taste

Instructions:

1. Preheat the oven to 200°C (180°C fan).
2. In a large bowl, toss the halved potatoes with olive oil, lemon juice, oregano, salt, and pepper.
3. Spread the potatoes on a baking tray in a single layer.
4. Roast for 15 minutes, or until golden and crispy, stirring halfway through.
5. Serve immediately.

Nutritional Information:
Kcal: 220 | Carb: 36g | Pro: 4g | Fat: 8g | Fib: 4g | Sod: 40mg

BALSAMIC GLAZED BRUSSELS SPROUTS

Prep Time: 5 minutes
Cook Time: 10 minutes
Difficulty: 2/10
Category: Gluten-Free, Vegetarian, Vegan

Ingredients:

- 200g Brussels sprouts, trimmed and halved
- 2 tbsp balsamic vinegar
- 1 tbsp olive oil
- 1 tsp honey (optional)
- Salt and pepper, to taste

Instructions:

1. Heat olive oil in a large pan over medium heat.
2. Add the Brussels sprouts, cut side down, and cook for 5-7 minutes until browned and tender.
3. Add the balsamic vinegar and honey (if using), and cook for an additional 2 minutes, stirring to coat.
4. Season with salt and pepper, and serve immediately.

Nutritional Information:
Kcal: 150 | Carb: 12g | Pro: 3g | Fat: 10g | Fib: 4g | Sod: 60mg

ROASTED BUTTERNUT SQUASH WITH SAGE

Prep Time: 5 minutes
Cook Time: 15 minutes
Difficulty: 2/10
Category: Gluten-Free, Vegetarian, Vegan

Ingredients:

- 400g butternut squash, peeled and diced
- 2 tbsp olive oil
- 1 tbsp fresh sage, chopped
- Salt and pepper, to taste

Instructions:

1. In a large bowl, toss the diced butternut squash with olive oil, sage, salt, and pepper.
2. Spread the squash on a baking tray in a single layer.
3. Roast for 15 minutes, or until tender and caramelised.
4. Serve immediately.

Nutritional Information:
Kcal: 180 | Carb: 26g | Pro: 2g | Fat: 8g | Fib: 6g | Sod: 40mg

SWEET POTATO WEDGES WITH SMOKED PAPRIKA

Prep Time: 5 minutes
Cook Time: 15 minutes
Difficulty: 2/10
Category: Gluten-Free, Vegetarian, Vegan

Ingredients:

- 400g sweet potatoes, cut into wedges
- 2 tbsp olive oil
- 1 tsp smoked paprika
- Salt and pepper, to taste

Instructions:

1. Preheat the oven to 200°C (180°C fan).
2. In a large bowl, toss the sweet potato wedges with olive oil, smoked paprika, salt, and pepper.
3. Spread the wedges on a baking tray in a single layer.
4. Roast for 15 minutes, or until tender and crispy, turning halfway through.
5. Serve immediately.

Nutritional Information:
Kcal: 220 | Carb: 36g | Pro: 3g | Fat: 8g | Fib: 6g | Sod: 60mg

SEAFOOD

GRILLED SALMON WITH LEMON AND DILL

Prep Time: 5 minutes
Cook Time: 10 minutes
Difficulty: 2/10
Category: Gluten-Free

Ingredients:

- 2 salmon fillets (about 150g each)
- 1 tbsp olive oil
- 1 lemon, sliced
- 1 tbsp fresh dill, chopped
- Salt and pepper, to taste

Instructions:

1. Preheat a grill or grill pan over medium heat and brush with olive oil.
2. Season the salmon fillets with salt and pepper.
3. Place the salmon fillets on the grill, skin-side down, and top each with lemon slices and chopped dill.
4. Grill for 4-5 minutes on each side, or until the salmon is cooked through.
5. Serve immediately with additional lemon wedges.

Nutritional Information:
Kcal: 350 | Carb: 2g | Pro: 34g | Fat: 24g | Fib: 1g | Sod: 90mg

GARLIC PRAWNS WITH OLIVE OIL AND PARSLEY

Prep Time: 5 minutes
Cook Time: 5 minutes
Difficulty: 2/10
Category: Gluten-Free

Ingredients:

- 200g prawns, peeled and deveined
- 2 garlic cloves, minced
- 2 tbsp olive oil
- 1 tbsp fresh parsley, chopped
- Juice of 1/2 lemon
- Salt and pepper, to taste

Instructions:

1. Heat olive oil in a large pan over medium heat.
2. Add the minced garlic and sauté for 1 minute until fragrant.
3. Add the prawns and cook for 2-3 minutes on each side until pink and opaque.
4. Stir in the lemon juice and chopped parsley, and season with salt and pepper.
5. Serve immediately.

Nutritional Information:
Kcal: 200 | Carb: 2g | Pro: 24g | Fat: 10g | Fib: 1g | Sod: 200mg

BAKED COD WITH TOMATOES AND OLIVES

Prep Time: 5 minutes
Cook Time: 10 minutes
Difficulty: 2/10
Category: Gluten-Free

Ingredients:

- 2 cod fillets (about 150g each)
- 1 can (400g) chopped tomatoes
- 10 Kalamata olives, pitted and halved
- 1 garlic clove, minced
- 1 tbsp olive oil
- 1 tsp dried oregano
- Salt and pepper, to taste

Instructions:

1. Preheat the oven to 200°C (180°C fan).
2. In a baking dish, combine the chopped tomatoes, olives, garlic, olive oil, oregano, salt, and pepper.
3. Place the cod fillets on top of the tomato mixture.
4. Bake for 10 minutes, or until the cod is cooked through and flakes easily with a fork.
5. Serve immediately.

Nutritional Information:
Kcal: 250 | Carb: 10g | Pro: 30g | Fat: 10g | Fib: 4g | Sod: 400mg

PAN-SEARED SEA BASS WITH CAPER SAUCE

Prep Time: 5 minutes
Cook Time: 10 minutes
Difficulty: 3/10
Category: Gluten-Free

Ingredients:

- 2 sea bass fillets (about 150g each)
- 2 tbsp olive oil
- 1 tbsp capers, rinsed
- 1 tbsp lemon juice
- 1 tbsp fresh parsley, chopped
- Salt and pepper, to taste

Instructions:

1. Heat olive oil in a large pan over medium-high heat.
2. Season the sea bass fillets with salt and pepper.
3. Place the fillets in the pan, skin-side down, and cook for 3-4 minutes until the skin is crispy.
4. Flip the fillets and cook for an additional 2-3 minutes until the fish is cooked through.
5. Remove the fillets from the pan and set aside.
6. In the same pan, add the capers, lemon juice, and parsley, and cook for 1 minute.
7. Pour the sauce over the sea bass fillets and serve immediately.

Nutritional Information:
Kcal: 300 | Carb: 2g | Pro: 32g | Fat: 18g | Fib: 1g | Sod: 500mg

MUSSELS IN WHITE WINE AND GARLIC

Prep Time: 5 minutes
Cook Time: 10 minutes
Difficulty: 3/10
Category: Gluten-Free

Ingredients:

- 500g fresh mussels, cleaned
- 2 garlic cloves, minced
- 1 shallot, finely chopped
- 200ml white wine
- 2 tbsp olive oil
- 1 tbsp fresh parsley, chopped
- Salt and pepper, to taste

Instructions:

1. Heat olive oil in a large pot over medium heat.
2. Add the garlic and shallot, and sauté for 2-3 minutes until softened.
3. Pour in the white wine and bring to a boil.
4. Add the mussels, cover the pot, and cook for 5-7 minutes, shaking the pot occasionally, until the mussels have opened.
5. Discard any mussels that remain closed.
6. Stir in the chopped parsley and season with salt and pepper.
7. Serve immediately with the cooking liquid.

Nutritional Information:
Kcal: 250 | Carb: 6g | Pro: 30g | Fat: 10g | Fib: 1g | Sod: 500mg

TUNA SALAD WITH OLIVES AND RED ONIONS

Prep Time: 5 minutes
Cook Time: None
Difficulty: 1/10
Category: Gluten-Free

Ingredients:

- 1 can (160g) tuna in olive oil, drained
- 10 Kalamata olives, pitted and halved
- 1/2 small red onion, thinly sliced
- 1 tbsp olive oil
- 1 tbsp lemon juice
- Salt and pepper, to taste

Instructions:

1. In a large bowl, combine the tuna, olives, and red onion.
2. Drizzle with olive oil and lemon juice.
3. Season with salt and pepper, and toss to combine.
4. Serve immediately.

Nutritional Information:
Kcal: 300 | Carb: 4g | Pro: 28g | Fat: 20g | Fib: 1g | Sod: 500mg

GRILLED SARDINES WITH LEMON AND HERBS

Prep Time: 5 minutes
Cook Time: 10 minutes
Difficulty: 2/10
Category: Gluten-Free

Ingredients:

- 6 fresh sardines, cleaned and gutted
- 2 tbsp olive oil
- Juice of 1 lemon
- 1 tbsp fresh parsley, chopped
- 1 tsp dried oregano
- Salt and pepper, to taste

Instructions:

1. Preheat a grill or grill pan over medium heat and brush with olive oil.
2. Season the sardines with salt, pepper, and dried oregano.
3. Grill the sardines for 3-4 minutes on each side until cooked through.
4. Drizzle with lemon juice and sprinkle with fresh parsley.
5. Serve immediately.

Nutritional Information:
Kcal: 300 | Carb: 2g | Pro: 25g | Fat: 20g | Fib: 0g | Sod: 400mg

MEDITERRANEAN FISH STEW WITH SAFFRON

Prep Time: 5 minutes
Cook Time: 10 minutes
Difficulty: 3/10
Category: Gluten-Free

Ingredients:

- 200g white fish fillets (such as cod or haddock), cut into chunks
- 1 small onion, chopped
- 2 garlic cloves, minced
- 1 can (400g) chopped tomatoes
- 200ml fish or vegetable broth
- 1/4 tsp saffron threads
- 1 tbsp olive oil
- 1 tbsp fresh parsley, chopped
- Salt and pepper, to taste

Instructions:

1. Heat olive oil in a large pot over medium heat.
2. Add the onion and garlic, and sauté for 3-4 minutes until softened.
3. Stir in the chopped tomatoes, broth, and saffron. Bring to a simmer.
4. Add the fish chunks and cook for 5-7 minutes until the fish is cooked through.
5. Season with salt and pepper, and stir in the fresh parsley.
6. Serve immediately.

Nutritional Information:
Kcal: 250 | Carb: 10g | Pro: 30g | Fat: 10g | Fib: 3g | Sod: 400mg

BAKED TROUT WITH ALMONDS AND HERBS

Prep Time: 5 minutes
Cook Time: 10 minutes
Difficulty: 2/10
Category: Gluten-Free

Ingredients:

- 2 trout fillets (about 150g each)
- 2 tbsp almonds, sliced
- 1 tbsp olive oil
- 1 tbsp fresh parsley, chopped
- Juice of 1/2 lemon
- Salt and pepper, to taste

Instructions:

1. Preheat the oven to 200°C (180°C fan).
2. Place the trout fillets on a baking tray lined with parchment paper.
3. Drizzle with olive oil and lemon juice, and season with salt and pepper.
4. Sprinkle the sliced almonds and chopped parsley over the trout.
5. Bake for 10 minutes, or until the trout is cooked through and the almonds are golden.
6. Serve immediately.

Nutritional Information:
Kcal: 350 | Carb: 2g | Pro: 32g | Fat: 24g | Fib: 2g | Sod: 150mg

GRILLED CALAMARI WITH LEMON AND GARLIC

Prep Time: 5 minutes
Cook Time: 5 minutes
Difficulty: 3/10
Category: Gluten-Free

Ingredients:

- 200g calamari, cleaned and sliced into rings
- 2 garlic cloves, minced
- 2 tbsp olive oil
- Juice of 1/2 lemon
- 1 tbsp fresh parsley, chopped
- Salt and pepper, to taste

Instructions:

1. Preheat a grill or grill pan over medium heat and brush with olive oil.
2. In a bowl, toss the calamari rings with garlic, olive oil, salt, and pepper.
3. Grill the calamari for 2-3 minutes on each side until tender.
4. Drizzle with lemon juice and sprinkle with fresh parsley.
5. Serve immediately.

Nutritional Information:
Kcal: 200 | Carb: 2g | Pro: 20g | Fat: 12g | Fib: 1g | Sod: 300mg

SPAGHETTI WITH CLAMS
(SPAGHETTI ALLE VONGOLE)

Prep Time: 5 minutes
Cook Time: 10 minutes
Difficulty: 3/10
Category: Gluten-Free (if using gluten-free pasta)

Ingredients:

- 150g spaghetti (use gluten-free if needed)
- 200g fresh clams, cleaned
- 2 garlic cloves, minced
- 1 small red chili, chopped
- 2 tbsp olive oil
- 1/4 cup white wine
- 1 tbsp fresh parsley, chopped
- Salt and pepper, to taste

Instructions:

1. Cook the spaghetti according to package instructions. Drain and set aside.
2. In a large pan, heat olive oil over medium heat. Add the garlic and chili, and sauté for 1 minute.
3. Add the clams and white wine, cover the pan, and cook for 5-7 minutes until the clams open.
4. Discard any clams that remain closed.
5. Add the cooked spaghetti to the pan, and toss to combine.
6. Season with salt and pepper, and stir in the fresh parsley.
7. Serve immediately.

Nutritional Information:
Kcal: 400 | Carb: 50g | Pro: 18g | Fat: 12g | Fib: 3g | Sod: 300mg

PRAWN AND AVOCADO SALAD

Prep Time: 5 minutes
Cook Time: None
Difficulty: 1/10
Category: Gluten-Free

Ingredients:

- 200g prawns, cooked and peeled
- 1 ripe avocado, diced
- 1 small cucumber, diced
- 10 cherry tomatoes, halved
- 2 tbsp olive oil
- Juice of 1/2 lemon
- Salt and pepper, to taste

Instructions:

1. In a large bowl, combine the prawns, avocado, cucumber, and cherry tomatoes.
2. Drizzle with olive oil and lemon juice.
3. Season with salt and pepper, and toss to combine.
4. Serve immediately.

Nutritional Information:
Kcal: 300 | Carb: 10g | Pro: 24g | Fat: 20g | Fib: 6g | Sod: 200mg

MEDITERRANEAN BAKED FISH WITH VEGETABLES

Prep Time: 10 minutes
Cook Time: 15 minutes
Difficulty: 3/10
Category: Gluten-Free

Ingredients:

- 2 white fish fillets (such as cod or haddock, about 150g each)
- 1 red pepper, sliced
- 1 courgette, sliced
- 1 small onion, sliced
- 10 cherry tomatoes, halved
- 2 tbsp olive oil
- 1 tsp dried oregano
- Salt and pepper, to taste

Instructions:

1. Preheat the oven to 200°C (180°C fan).
2. In a baking dish, arrange the sliced vegetables and drizzle with olive oil. Season with salt, pepper, and oregano.
3. Place the fish fillets on top of the vegetables and drizzle with a little more olive oil.
4. Bake for 15 minutes, or until the fish is cooked through and the vegetables are tender.
5. Serve immediately.

Nutritional Information:
Kcal: 320 | Carb: 10g | Pro: 34g | Fat: 18g | Fib: 4g | Sod: 200mg

SMOKED MACKEREL PÂTÉ

Prep Time: 5 minutes
Cook Time: None
Difficulty: 2/10
Category: Gluten-Free

Ingredients:

- 150g smoked mackerel fillets, skin removed
- 100g cream cheese
- 1 tbsp lemon juice
- 1 tbsp fresh chives, chopped
- Salt and pepper, to taste

Instructions:

1. In a food processor, combine the smoked mackerel, cream cheese, and lemon juice.
2. Blend until smooth.
3. Stir in the chopped chives and season with salt and pepper.
4. Serve immediately or refrigerate until needed.

Nutritional Information:
Kcal: 300 | Carb: 2g | Pro: 20g | Fat: 24g | Fib: 0g | Sod: 400mg

SHRIMP AND TOMATO SKEWERS

Prep Time: 5 minutes
Cook Time: 10 minutes
Difficulty: 2/10
Category: Gluten-Free

Ingredients:

- 200g shrimp, peeled and deveined
- 10 cherry tomatoes
- 2 tbsp olive oil
- 1 tbsp lemon juice
- 1 garlic clove, minced
- Salt and pepper, to taste

Instructions:

1. Preheat a grill or grill pan over medium heat.
2. In a bowl, toss the shrimp and cherry tomatoes with olive oil, lemon juice, garlic, salt, and pepper.
3. Thread the shrimp and tomatoes onto skewers.
4. Grill the skewers for 2-3 minutes on each side until the shrimp are cooked through.
5. Serve immediately.

Nutritional Information:
Kcal: 220 | Carb: 4g | Pro: 24g | Fat: 12g | Fib: 1g | Sod: 200mg

SEAFOOD PAELLA WITH SAFFRON

Prep Time: 10 minutes
Cook Time: 15 minutes
Difficulty: 4/10
Category: Gluten-Free

Ingredients:

- 100g paella rice
- 200g mixed seafood (prawns, mussels, squid)
- 1 small onion, chopped
- 1 garlic clove, minced
- 1/4 tsp saffron threads
- 400ml fish or vegetable broth
- 2 tbsp olive oil
- 1 red pepper, sliced
- Salt and pepper, to taste

Instructions:

1. Heat olive oil in a large pan over medium heat. Add the onion, garlic, and red pepper, and sauté for 3-4 minutes until softened.
2. Stir in the paella rice and saffron, and cook for 1 minute to toast the rice.
3. Add the broth and bring to a simmer.
4. Add the mixed seafood and cook for 10-12 minutes until the rice is tender and the seafood is cooked through.
5. Season with salt and pepper, and serve immediately.

Nutritional Information:
Kcal: 350 | Carb: 50g | Pro: 24g | Fat: 8g | Fib: 3g | Sod: 300mg

OVEN-BAKED SCALLOPS WITH LEMON AND GARLIC

Prep Time: 5 minutes
Cook Time: 10 minutes
Difficulty: 2/10
Category: Gluten-Free

Ingredients:

- 200g scallops, cleaned
- 2 garlic cloves, minced
- 2 tbsp olive oil
- Juice of 1/2 lemon
- Salt and pepper, to taste

Instructions:

1. Preheat the oven to 200°C (180°C fan).
2. In a baking dish, arrange the scallops and drizzle with olive oil and lemon juice.
3. Sprinkle with minced garlic, salt, and pepper.
4. Bake for 10 minutes, or until the scallops are cooked through and slightly golden.
5. Serve immediately.

Nutritional Information:
Kcal: 220 | Carb: 4g | Pro: 20g | Fat: 14g | Fib: 0g | Sod: 200mg

GRILLED TUNA STEAK WITH FRESH HERBS

Prep Time: 5 minutes
Cook Time: 5 minutes
Difficulty: 3/10
Category: Gluten-Free

Ingredients:

- 2 tuna steaks (about 150g each)
- 2 tbsp olive oil
- 1 tbsp fresh parsley, chopped
- 1 tbsp fresh basil, chopped
- Juice of 1/2 lemon
- Salt and pepper, to taste

Instructions:

1. Preheat a grill or grill pan over medium-high heat and brush with olive oil.
2. Season the tuna steaks with salt, pepper, and lemon juice.
3. Grill the tuna steaks for 2-3 minutes on each side for medium-rare, or longer for desired doneness.
4. Remove from the grill and sprinkle with fresh herbs.
5. Serve immediately.

Nutritional Information:
Kcal: 300 | Carb: 2g | Pro: 34g | Fat: 18g | Fib: 1g | Sod: 200mg

ANCHOVY AND GARLIC BRUSCHETTA

Prep Time: 5 minutes
Cook Time: 5 minutes
Difficulty: 2/10
Category: Gluten-Free (if using gluten-free bread)

Ingredients:

- 4 slices of crusty bread (use gluten-free if needed)
- 4 anchovy fillets
- 2 garlic cloves, halved
- 2 tbsp olive oil
- 1 tbsp fresh parsley, chopped

Instructions:

1. Toast the bread slices until golden and crispy.
2. Rub the toasted bread with the cut sides of the garlic cloves.
3. Top each slice with an anchovy fillet.
4. Drizzle with olive oil and sprinkle with fresh parsley.
5. Serve immediately.

Nutritional Information:
Kcal: 220 | Carb: 20g | Pro: 6g | Fat: 14g | Fib: 2g | Sod: 500mg

BAKED SALMON WITH A MUSTARD-DILL GLAZE

Prep Time: 5 minutes
Cook Time: 10 minutes
Difficulty: 2/10
Category: Gluten-Free

Ingredients:

- 2 salmon fillets (about 150g each)
- 2 tbsp Dijon mustard
- 1 tbsp honey
- 1 tbsp fresh dill, chopped
- 1 tbsp olive oil
- Salt and pepper, to taste

Instructions:

1. Preheat the oven to 200°C (180°C fan).
2. In a small bowl, mix the Dijon mustard, honey, fresh dill, olive oil, salt, and pepper.
3. Place the salmon fillets on a baking tray lined with parchment paper.
4. Spread the mustard-dill glaze over the top of each fillet.
5. Bake for 10 minutes, or until the salmon is cooked through.
6. Serve immediately.

Nutritional Information:
Kcal: 350 | Carb: 6g | Pro: 34g | Fat: 20g | Fib: 1g | Sod: 200mg

MEAT

GRILLED CHICKEN SOUVLAKI WITH TZATZIKI

Prep Time: 10 minutes
Cook Time: 10 minutes
Difficulty: 3/10
Category: Gluten-Free

Ingredients:

- 2 chicken breasts, cut into cubes
- 2 tbsp olive oil
- 1 tbsp lemon juice
- 1 garlic clove, minced
- 1 tsp dried oregano
- Salt and pepper, to taste

For the Tzatziki:

- 100g Greek yogurt
- 1/2 cucumber, grated and drained
- 1 garlic clove, minced
- 1 tbsp lemon juice
- Salt, to taste

Instructions:

1. In a bowl, combine the olive oil, lemon juice, garlic, oregano, salt, and pepper. Add the chicken cubes and marinate for at least 10 minutes.
2. Thread the marinated chicken onto skewers.
3. Preheat a grill or grill pan over medium heat.
4. Grill the chicken skewers for 4-5 minutes on each side, or until cooked through.
5. In a small bowl, mix all the ingredients for the tzatziki.
6. Serve the chicken souvlaki with the tzatziki on the side.

Nutritional Information:
Kcal: 300 | Carb: 5g | Pro: 36g | Fat: 14g | Fib: 1g | Sod: 200mg

LAMB KOFTA WITH MINT YOGURT

Prep Time: 10 minutes
Cook Time: 10 minutes
Difficulty: 3/10
Category: Gluten-Free

Ingredients:

- 200g ground lamb
- 1 garlic clove, minced
- 1 small onion, grated
- 1 tsp ground cumin
- 1 tsp ground coriander
- 1 tbsp fresh mint, chopped
- Salt and pepper, to taste
- For the Mint Yogurt:
- 100g Greek yogurt
- 1 tbsp fresh mint, chopped
- 1 tbsp lemon juice
- Salt, to taste

Instructions:

1. In a bowl, mix the ground lamb, garlic, grated onion, cumin, coriander, mint, salt, and pepper.
2. Form the mixture into small oval-shaped patties.
3. Preheat a grill or grill pan over medium heat.
4. Grill the kofta for 4-5 minutes on each side, or until cooked through.
5. In a small bowl, mix all the ingredients for the mint yogurt.
6. Serve the lamb kofta with the mint yogurt on the side.

Nutritional Information:
Kcal: 350 | Carb: 4g | Pro: 22g | Fat: 28g | Fib: 1g | Sod: 200mg

BAKED CHICKEN THIGHS WITH OLIVES AND LEMON

Prep Time: 5 minutes
Cook Time: 15 minutes
Difficulty: 2/10
Category: Gluten-Free

Ingredients:

- 4 chicken thighs, bone-in and skin-on
- 2 tbsp olive oil
- Juice of 1 lemon
- 10 Kalamata olives, pitted and halved
- 1 garlic clove, minced
- 1 tsp dried oregano
- Salt and pepper, to taste

Instructions:

1. Preheat the oven to 200°C (180°C fan).
2. In a baking dish, arrange the chicken thighs, skin-side up.
3. Drizzle with olive oil and lemon juice, and sprinkle with garlic, oregano, salt, and pepper.
4. Scatter the olives around the chicken thighs.
5. Bake for 15 minutes, or until the chicken is cooked through and the skin is crispy.
6. Serve immediately.

Nutritional Information:
Kcal: 400 | Carb: 2g | Pro: 30g | Fat: 30g | Fib: 0g | Sod: 400mg

BEEF AND VEGETABLE KEBABS

Prep Time: 10 minutes
Cook Time: 10 minutes
Difficulty: 3/10
Category: Gluten-Free

Ingredients:

- 200g beef sirloin, cut into cubes
- 1 red pepper, cut into chunks
- 1 courgette, sliced
- 1 red onion, cut into chunks
- 2 tbsp olive oil
- 1 tbsp balsamic vinegar
- 1 garlic clove, minced
- 1 tsp dried thyme
- Salt and pepper, to taste

Instructions:

1. In a bowl, combine the olive oil, balsamic vinegar, garlic, thyme, salt, and pepper. Add the beef cubes and marinate for at least 10 minutes.
2. Thread the beef and vegetables onto skewers.
3. Preheat a grill or grill pan over medium heat.
4. Grill the kebabs for 4-5 minutes on each side, or until the beef is cooked to your liking.
5. Serve immediately.

Nutritional Information:
Kcal: 350 | Carb: 8g | Pro: 28g | Fat: 24g | Fib: 2g | Sod: 200mg

SLOW-COOKED LAMB SHOULDER WITH ROSEMARY

Prep Time: 10 minutes
Cook Time: 15 min. (active), 3 h. (slow-cooking)
Difficulty: 4/10
Category: Gluten-Free

Ingredients:

- 500g lamb shoulder, bone-in
- 2 garlic cloves, minced
- 2 sprigs fresh rosemary
- 2 tbsp olive oil
- Juice of 1 lemon
- 200ml lamb or vegetable broth
- Salt and pepper, to taste

Instructions:

1. Preheat the oven to 160°C (140°C fan).
2. In a roasting pan, rub the lamb shoulder with garlic, rosemary, olive oil, lemon juice, salt, and pepper.
3. Add the broth to the pan and cover tightly with foil.
4. Slow-cook in the oven for 3 hours, or until the lamb is tender and falls off the bone.
5. Serve immediately with the pan juices.

Nutritional Information:
Kcal: 450 | Carb: 2g | Pro: 30g | Fat: 34g | Fib: 0g | Sod: 300mg

MEDITERRANEAN CHICKEN STEW WITH TOMATOES AND OLIVES

Prep Time: 10 minutes
Cook Time: 15 minutes
Difficulty: 3/10
Category: Gluten-Free

Ingredients:

- 2 chicken breasts, cut into cubes
- 1 can (400g) chopped tomatoes
- 10 Kalamata olives, pitted and halved
- 1 small onion, chopped
- 2 garlic cloves, minced
- 1 tsp dried oregano
- 2 tbsp olive oil
- Salt and pepper, to taste

Instructions:

1. Heat olive oil in a large pot over medium heat. Add the onion and garlic, and sauté for 3-4 minutes until softened.
2. Add the chicken cubes and cook until browned, about 5 minutes.
3. Stir in the chopped tomatoes, olives, oregano, salt, and pepper.
4. Bring to a simmer and cook for another 10 minutes until the chicken is cooked through and the sauce thickens.
5. Serve immediately.

Nutritional Information:
Kcal: 320 | Carb: 10g | Pro: 36g | Fat: 16g | Fib: 3g | Sod: 400mg

PORK TENDERLOIN WITH GARLIC AND THYME

Prep Time: 5 minutes
Cook Time: 10 minutes
Difficulty: 2/10
Category: Gluten-Free

Ingredients:

- 300g pork tenderloin, trimmed and cut into medallions
- 2 garlic cloves, minced
- 1 tsp dried thyme
- 2 tbsp olive oil
- Salt and pepper, to taste

Instructions:

1. Season the pork medallions with garlic, thyme, salt, and pepper.
2. Heat olive oil in a large pan over medium-high heat.
3. Add the pork medallions and cook for 3-4 minutes on each side, until browned and cooked through.
4. Serve immediately with pan juices.

Nutritional Information:
Kcal: 300 | Carb: 2g | Pro: 32g | Fat: 18g | Fib: 0g | Sod: 200mg

STUFFED CHICKEN BREAST WITH SPINACH AND FETA

Prep Time: 10 minutes
Cook Time: 15 minutes
Difficulty: 3/10
Category: Gluten-Free

Ingredients:

- 2 chicken breasts
- 100g spinach, washed
- 50g feta cheese, crumbled
- 2 garlic cloves, minced
- 2 tbsp olive oil
- Salt and pepper, to taste

Instructions:

1. Preheat the oven to 200°C (180°C fan).
2. Butterfly the chicken breasts and stuff with spinach, feta cheese, and garlic. Secure with toothpicks.
3. Heat olive oil in a pan over medium-high heat. Sear the chicken breasts for 2-3 minutes on each side.
4. Transfer to a baking dish and bake for 10 minutes, or until the chicken is cooked through.
5. Serve immediately.

Nutritional Information:
Kcal: 350 | Carb: 2g | Pro: 40g | Fat: 20g | Fib: 1g | Sod: 400mg

GREEK MEATBALLS (KEFTEDES) WITH TOMATO SAUCE

Prep Time: 10 minutes
Cook Time: 15 minutes
Difficulty: 3/10
Category: Gluten-Free

Ingredients:

- 200g ground beef
- 1 small onion, grated
- 1 garlic clove, minced
- 1 tsp dried oregano
- 1 egg, beaten
- 2 tbsp olive oil
- 1 can (400g) chopped tomatoes
- Salt and pepper, to taste

Instructions:

1. In a bowl, mix the ground beef, grated onion, garlic, oregano, beaten egg, salt, and pepper. Form into small meatballs.
2. Heat olive oil in a large pan over medium heat. Brown the meatballs on all sides, about 5 minutes.
3. Add the chopped tomatoes to the pan and simmer for 10 minutes until the sauce thickens and the meatballs are cooked through.
4. Serve immediately.

Nutritional Information:
Kcal: 350 | Carb: 8g | Pro: 28g | Fat: 24g | Fib: 2g | Sod: 400mg

ROAST LEG OF LAMB WITH GARLIC AND HERBS

Prep Time: 10 minutes
Cook Time: 15 min. (active), 1.5 h. (roasting)
Difficulty: 4/10
Category: Gluten-Free

Ingredients:

- 1kg leg of lamb
- 4 garlic cloves, sliced
- 2 sprigs fresh rosemary
- 2 tbsp olive oil
- Juice of 1 lemon
- Salt and pepper, to taste

Instructions:

1. Preheat the oven to 180°C (160°C fan).
2. Make small slits in the lamb and insert garlic slices and rosemary sprigs.
3. Rub the lamb with olive oil, lemon juice, salt, and pepper.
4. Place the lamb in a roasting pan and roast for 1.5 hours, or until the lamb is cooked to your liking.
5. Let the lamb rest for 10 minutes before carving.
6. Serve with pan juices.

Nutritional Information:
Kcal: 500 | Carb: 2g | Pro: 40g | Fat: 36g | Fib: 0g | Sod: 300mg

GRILLED PORK CHOPS WITH ROSEMARY AND LEMON

Prep Time: 5 minutes
Cook Time: 10 minutes
Difficulty: 2/10
Category: Gluten-Free

Ingredients:

- 2 pork chops (about 150g each)
- 2 tbsp olive oil
- Juice of 1 lemon
- 1 tsp dried rosemary
- Salt and pepper, to taste

Instructions:

1. Preheat a grill or grill pan over medium heat and brush with olive oil.
2. Rub the pork chops with lemon juice, rosemary, salt, and pepper.
3. Grill the pork chops for 4-5 minutes on each side, or until cooked through.
4. Serve immediately with additional lemon wedges.

Nutritional Information:
Kcal: 350 | Carb: 2g | Pro: 34g | Fat: 22g | Fib: 0g | Sod: 200mg

CHICKEN TAGINE WITH APRICOTS AND ALMONDS

Prep Time: 10 minutes
Cook Time: 15 minutes
Difficulty: 4/10
Category: Gluten-Free

Ingredients:

- 2 chicken breasts, cut into cubes
- 1 small onion, chopped
- 2 garlic cloves, minced
- 50g dried apricots, chopped
- 1 tsp ground cumin
- 1 tsp ground cinnamon
- 2 tbsp olive oil
- 200ml chicken broth
- 20g almonds, toasted
- Salt and pepper, to taste

Instructions:

1. Heat olive oil in a large pan over medium heat. Add the onion and garlic, and sauté for 3-4 minutes until softened.
2. Add the chicken cubes, cumin, and cinnamon, and cook for 5 minutes until browned.
3. Stir in the chopped apricots and chicken broth. Bring to a simmer and cook for 10 minutes until the chicken is cooked through and the sauce thickens.
4. Garnish with toasted almonds and serve immediately.

Nutritional Information:
Kcal: 350 | Carb: 20g | Pro: 36g | Fat: 14g | Fib: 4g | Sod: 300mg

BEEF MOUSSAKA WITH AUBERGINES

Prep Time: 10 minutes
Cook Time: 20 minutes
Difficulty: 4/10
Category: Gluten-Free

Ingredients:

- 200g ground beef
- 1 large aubergine, sliced
- 1 small onion, chopped
- 2 garlic cloves, minced
- 1 can (400g) chopped tomatoes
- 1 tsp ground cinnamon
- 2 tbsp olive oil
- Salt and pepper, to taste
- 50g grated Parmesan cheese (optional)

Instructions:

1. Preheat the oven to 200°C (180°C fan).
2. In a pan, heat 1 tablespoon of olive oil over medium heat. Add the aubergine slices and cook until soft, about 5 minutes. Set aside.
3. In the same pan, add the remaining olive oil and sauté the onion and garlic for 3-4 minutes until softened.
4. Add the ground beef, cinnamon, salt, and pepper, and cook until browned, about 5 minutes.
5. Stir in the chopped tomatoes and simmer for 10 minutes.
6. In a baking dish, layer the aubergine slices and beef mixture. Top with grated Parmesan if desired.
7. Bake for 15 minutes, or until the top is golden and bubbly.
8. Serve immediately.

Nutritional Information:
Kcal: 400 | Carb: 12g | Pro: 28g | Fat: 28g | Fib: 4g | Sod: 400mg

BRAISED BEEF WITH RED WINE AND ROSEMARY

Prep Time: 10 minutes
Cook Time: 15 min. (active), 2 h. (braising)
Difficulty: 4/10
Category: Gluten-Free

Ingredients:

- 500g beef stewing steak, cut into cubes
- 1 small onion, chopped
- 2 garlic cloves, minced
- 200ml red wine
- 2 sprigs fresh rosemary
- 2 tbsp olive oil
- 200ml beef broth
- Salt and pepper, to taste

Instructions:

1. Preheat the oven to 160°C (140°C fan).
2. In a large pan, heat olive oil over medium heat. Brown the beef cubes on all sides, about 5 minutes.
3. Add the onion and garlic, and sauté for 3-4 minutes until softened.
4. Pour in the red wine and beef broth, and add the rosemary sprigs.
5. Bring to a simmer, then transfer to a baking dish and cover tightly with foil.
6. Braise in the oven for 2 hours, or until the beef is tender.
7. Serve immediately with the braising liquid.

Nutritional Information:
Kcal: 450 | Carb: 4g | Pro: 40g | Fat: 28g | Fib: 0g | Sod: 400mg

CHICKEN CACCIATORE WITH MUSHROOMS AND PEPPERS

Prep Time: 10 minutes
Cook Time: 15 minutes
Difficulty: 3/10
Category: Gluten-Free

Ingredients:

- 2 chicken breasts, cut into cubes
- 1 small onion, chopped
- 1 red pepper, sliced
- 100g mushrooms, sliced
- 2 garlic cloves, minced
- 1 can (400g) chopped tomatoes
- 1 tsp dried oregano
- 2 tbsp olive oil
- Salt and pepper, to taste

Instructions:

1. Heat olive oil in a large pan over medium heat. Add the onion, garlic, red pepper, and mushrooms, and sauté for 3-4 minutes until softened.
2. Add the chicken cubes and cook until browned, about 5 minutes.
3. Stir in the chopped tomatoes, oregano, salt, and pepper.
4. Bring to a simmer and cook for another 10 minutes until the chicken is cooked through and the sauce thickens.
5. Serve immediately.

Nutritional Information:
Kcal: 320 | Carb: 12g | Pro: 36g | Fat: 14g | Fib: 4g | Sod: 400mg

SPICY LAMB MEATBALLS WITH HARISSA

Prep Time: 10 minutes
Cook Time: 15 minutes
Difficulty: 3/10
Category: Gluten-Free

Ingredients:

- 200g ground lamb
- 1 small onion, grated
- 1 garlic clove, minced
- 1 tbsp harissa paste
- 1 egg, beaten
- 2 tbsp olive oil
- Salt and pepper, to taste

Instructions:

1. In a bowl, mix the ground lamb, grated onion, garlic, harissa paste, beaten egg, salt, and pepper. Form into small meatballs.
2. Heat olive oil in a large pan over medium heat. Brown the meatballs on all sides, about 5 minutes.
3. Cover and cook for an additional 10 minutes until the meatballs are cooked through.
4. Serve immediately.

Nutritional Information:
Kcal: 350 | Carb: 4g | Pro: 28g | Fat: 24g | Fib: 1g | Sod: 400mg

ROAST CHICKEN WITH MEDITERRANEAN VEGETABLES

Prep Time: 10 minutes
Cook Time: 15 minutes
Difficulty: 3/10
Category: Gluten-Free

Ingredients:

- 2 chicken breasts, skin-on
- 1 red pepper, sliced
- 1 courgette, sliced
- 1 small onion, sliced
- 10 cherry tomatoes, halved
- 2 tbsp olive oil
- 1 tsp dried oregano
- Salt and pepper, to taste

Instructions:

1. Preheat the oven to 200°C (180°C fan).
2. In a baking dish, arrange the sliced vegetables and drizzle with olive oil. Season with salt, pepper, and oregano.
3. Place the chicken breasts on top of the vegetables and drizzle with a little more olive oil.
4. Roast for 15 minutes, or until the chicken is cooked through and the vegetables are tender.
5. Serve immediately.

Nutritional Information:
Kcal: 350 | Carb: 10g | Pro: 36g | Fat: 18g | Fib: 4g | Sod: 200mg

BEEF AND TOMATO STEW WITH CINNAMON

Prep Time: 10 minutes
Cook Time: 15 min. (active), 1 h. (simmering)
Difficulty: 4/10
Category: Gluten-Free

Ingredients:

- 500g beef stewing steak, cut into cubes
- 1 small onion, chopped
- 2 garlic cloves, minced
- 1 can (400g) chopped tomatoes
- 1 tsp ground cinnamon
- 2 tbsp olive oil
- 200ml beef broth
- Salt and pepper, to taste

Instructions:

1. In a large pot, heat olive oil over medium heat. Brown the beef cubes on all sides, about 5 minutes.
2. Add the onion and garlic, and sauté for 3-4 minutes until softened.
3. Stir in the chopped tomatoes, beef broth, and cinnamon.
4. Bring to a simmer, then cover and cook for 1 hour, or until the beef is tender.
5. Season with salt and pepper, and serve immediately.

Nutritional Information:
Kcal: 450 | Carb: 10g | Pro: 40g | Fat: 28g | Fib: 2g | Sod: 400mg

MARINATED GRILLED LAMB CHOPS

Prep Time: 10 minutes
Cook Time: 10 minutes
Difficulty: 3/10
Category: Gluten-Free

Ingredients:

- 4 lamb chops
- 2 tbsp olive oil
- Juice of 1 lemon
- 2 garlic cloves, minced
- 1 tsp dried rosemary
- Salt and pepper, to taste

Instructions:

1. In a bowl, mix the olive oil, lemon juice, garlic, rosemary, salt, and pepper. Add the lamb chops and marinate for at least 10 minutes.
2. Preheat a grill or grill pan over medium-high heat.
3. Grill the lamb chops for 4-5 minutes on each side, or until cooked to your liking.
4. Serve immediately.

Nutritional Information:
Kcal: 400 | Carb: 2g | Pro: 30g | Fat: 30g | Fib: 0g | Sod: 300mg

STUFFED PEPPERS WITH GROUND BEEF AND RICE

Prep Time: 10 minutes
Cook Time: 15 minutes
Difficulty: 3/10
Category: Gluten-Free

Ingredients:

- 2 large bell peppers, halved and seeded
- 200g ground beef
- 100g cooked rice
- 1 small onion, chopped
- 2 garlic cloves, minced
- 1 can (400g) chopped tomatoes
- 2 tbsp olive oil
- 1 tsp dried oregano
- Salt and pepper, to taste

Instructions:

1. Preheat the oven to 200°C (180°C fan).
2. In a pan, heat olive oil over medium heat. Add the onion and garlic, and sauté for 3-4 minutes until softened.
3. Add the ground beef and cook until browned, about 5 minutes.
4. Stir in the cooked rice, chopped tomatoes, oregano, salt, and pepper.
5. Stuff the pepper halves with the beef and rice mixture, and place them in a baking dish.
6. Bake for 15 minutes, or until the peppers are tender.
7. Serve immediately.

Nutritional Information:
Kcal: 350 | Carb: 20g | Pro: 28g | Fat: 18g | Fib: 4g | Sod: 400mg

DESSERTS

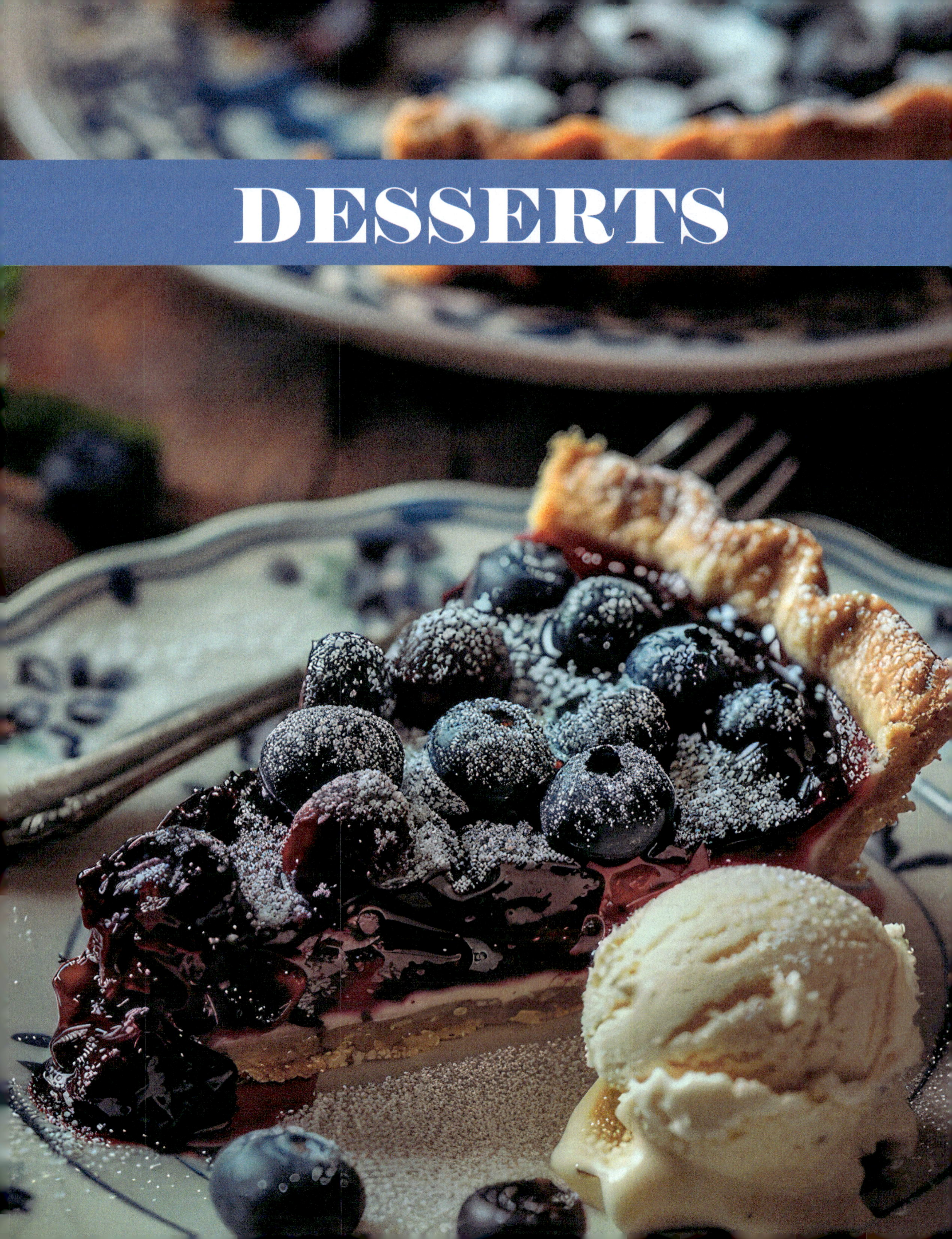

GREEK YOGURT WITH HONEY AND WALNUTS

Prep Time: 5 minutes
Cook Time: None
Difficulty: 1/10
Category: Gluten-Free, Vegetarian

Ingredients:

- 200g Greek yogurt
- 2 tbsp honey
- 2 tbsp walnuts, chopped
- 1/2 tsp ground cinnamon (optional)

Instructions:

1. Spoon the Greek yogurt into two serving bowls.
2. Drizzle each bowl with honey.
3. Sprinkle with chopped walnuts and ground cinnamon, if using.
4. Serve immediately.

Nutritional Information:
Kcal: 220 | Carb: 20g | Pro: 10g | Fat: 12g | Fib: 2g | Sod: 60mg

OLIVE OIL AND ALMOND CAKE

Prep Time: 10 minutes
Cook Time: 20 minutes
Difficulty: 3/10
Category: Gluten-Free, Vegetarian

Ingredients:

- 100g ground almonds
- 50g plain flour (use gluten-free if necessary)
- 100g sugar
- 2 eggs
- 50ml olive oil
- Zest of 1 lemon
- 1/2 tsp baking powder
- Pinch of salt

Instructions:

1. Preheat the oven to 180°C (160°C fan). Grease a small cake tin.
2. In a bowl, whisk together the eggs and sugar until pale and fluffy.
3. Add the olive oil, lemon zest, and ground almonds, and mix until combined.
4. Sift in the flour, baking powder, and salt, and fold gently into the mixture.
5. Pour the batter into the prepared cake tin and bake for 20 minutes, or until a skewer inserted into the center comes out clean.
6. Let cool before serving.

Nutritional Information:
Kcal: 320 | Carb: 28g | Pro: 6g | Fat: 20g | Fib: 2g | Sod: 100mg

LEMON SORBET WITH FRESH MINT

Prep Time: 5 minutes (plus freezing time)
Cook Time: None
Difficulty: 2/10
Category: Gluten-Free, Vegetarian, Vegan

Ingredients:

- 100ml fresh lemon juice
- 50g sugar
- 150ml water
- Fresh mint leaves, for garnish

Instructions:

1. In a small saucepan, heat the water and sugar over low heat until the sugar dissolves. Let cool.
2. Stir in the lemon juice and pour the mixture into a shallow container.
3. Freeze for 3-4 hours, stirring every hour to break up ice crystals.
4. Serve in bowls, garnished with fresh mint leaves.

Nutritional Information:
Kcal: 100 | Carb: 26g | Pro: 0g | Fat: 0g | Fib: 1g | Sod: 0mg

BAKLAVA WITH PISTACHIOS AND HONEY

Prep Time: 10 minutes
Cook Time: 15 minutes
Difficulty: 4/10
Category: Vegetarian

Ingredients:

- 100g phyllo pastry sheets, thawed
- 50g pistachios, chopped
- 50g walnuts, chopped
- 50g butter, melted
- 2 tbsp honey
- 1/2 tsp ground cinnamon

Instructions:

1. Preheat the oven to 180°C (160°C fan). Grease a small baking dish.
2. In a bowl, mix the chopped pistachios, walnuts, and cinnamon.
3. Layer two phyllo sheets in the baking dish, brushing each with melted butter.
4. Sprinkle a third of the nut mixture over the phyllo.
5. Repeat the layers twice more, finishing with a layer of phyllo sheets brushed with butter.
6. Cut into small squares and bake for 15 minutes, or until golden.
7. Drizzle with honey and let cool before serving.

Nutritional Information:
Kcal: 300 | Carb: 35g | Pro: 5g | Fat: 18g | Fib: 3g | Sod: 120mg

ALMOND AND ORANGE CAKE

Prep Time: 10 minutes
Cook Time: 25 minutes
Difficulty: 3/10
Category: Gluten-Free, Vegetarian

Ingredients:

- 100g ground almonds
- 2 eggs
- 100g sugar
- 50ml olive oil
- Zest and juice of 1 orange
- 1/2 tsp baking powder

Instructions:

1. Preheat the oven to 180°C (160°C fan). Grease a small cake tin.
2. In a bowl, whisk the eggs and sugar until pale and fluffy.
3. Add the olive oil, orange zest, and juice, and mix well.
4. Fold in the ground almonds and baking powder.
5. Pour the batter into the prepared cake tin and bake for 25 minutes, or until a skewer inserted into the center comes out clean.
6. Let cool before serving.

Nutritional Information:
Kcal: 300 | Carb: 28g | Pro: 6g | Fat: 18g | Fib: 2g | Sod: 100mg

GREEK RICE PUDDING (RIZOGALO)

Prep Time: 5 minutes
Cook Time: 15 minutes
Difficulty: 2/10
Category: Gluten-Free, Vegetarian

Ingredients:

- 100g short-grain rice
- 500ml milk (use almond milk for dairy-free)
- 50g sugar
- 1 cinnamon stick
- Zest of 1 lemon
- Ground cinnamon, for garnish

Instructions:

1. In a saucepan, combine the rice, milk, sugar, cinnamon stick, and lemon zest.
2. Bring to a simmer over medium heat, stirring occasionally.
3. Reduce the heat and cook for 15 minutes, or until the rice is tender and the mixture thickens.
4. Remove the cinnamon stick and divide the pudding into bowls.
5. Garnish with ground cinnamon and serve warm or chilled.

Nutritional Information:
Kcal: 200 | Carb: 40g | Pro: 5g | Fat: 4g | Fib: 1g | Sod: 50mg

FRESH FRUIT SALAD WITH LEMON AND HONEY

Prep Time: 5 minutes
Cook Time: None
Difficulty: 1/10
Category: Gluten-Free, Vegetarian, Vegan

Ingredients:

- 1 orange, segmented
- 1 apple, diced
- 1 kiwi, sliced
- 1 handful of berries (e.g., strawberries, blueberries)
- Juice of 1/2 lemon
- 1 tbsp honey (optional)

Instructions:

1. In a large bowl, combine all the fruit.
2. Drizzle with lemon juice and honey, if using.
3. Toss gently to combine.
4. Serve immediately.

Nutritional Information:
Kcal: 150 | Carb: 36g | Pro: 2g | Fat: 1g | Fib: 6g | Sod: 10mg

FIG AND WALNUT BARS

Prep Time: 10 minutes
Cook Time: 10 minutes (plus chilling time)
Difficulty: 3/10
Category: Gluten-Free, Vegetarian

Ingredients:

- 100g dried figs, chopped
- 50g walnuts, chopped
- 50g oats (use gluten-free if necessary)
- 2 tbsp honey
- 1 tbsp almond butter
- 1 tsp vanilla extract

Instructions:

1. In a food processor, blend the figs, walnuts, oats, honey, almond butter, and vanilla until a sticky dough forms.
2. Press the mixture into a small baking dish lined with parchment paper.
3. Chill in the fridge for at least 1 hour.
4. Cut into bars and serve.

Nutritional Information:
Kcal: 220 | Carb: 32g | Pro: 4g | Fat: 10g | Fib: 4g | Sod: 10mg

RICOTTA CHEESECAKE WITH LEMON ZEST

Prep Time: 10 minutes
Cook Time: 15 minutes
Difficulty: 3/10
Category: Gluten-Free, Vegetarian

Ingredients:

- 200g ricotta cheese
- 50g sugar
- Zest of 1 lemon
- 1 egg
- 1/2 tsp vanilla extract

Instructions:

1. Preheat the oven to 180°C (160°C fan). Grease a small cake tin.
2. In a bowl, mix the ricotta, sugar, lemon zest, egg, and vanilla until smooth.
3. Pour the mixture into the prepared tin.
4. Bake for 15 minutes, or until the cheesecake is set and slightly golden.
5. Let cool before serving.

Nutritional Information:
Kcal: 250 | Carb: 24g | Pro: 10g | Fat: 14g | Fib: 0g | Sod: 120mg

APRICOT AND ALMOND TART

Prep Time: 10 minutes
Cook Time: 20 minutes
Difficulty: 3/10
Category: Vegetarian

Ingredients:

- 100g shortcrust pastry (use gluten-free if necessary)
- 50g ground almonds
- 50g sugar
- 50g butter, softened
- 4 apricots, halved
- 1 egg

Instructions:

1. Preheat the oven to 180°C (160°C fan). Grease a small tart tin.
2. Roll out the pastry and line the tart tin.
3. In a bowl, cream the butter and sugar together until light and fluffy.
4. Beat in the egg, then fold in the ground almonds.
5. Spread the almond mixture over the pastry base.
6. Arrange the apricot halves on top, cut side up.
7. Bake for 20 minutes, or until the tart is golden and set.
8. Let cool before serving.

Nutritional Information:
Kcal: 350 | Carb: 40g | Pro: 6g | Fat: 18g | Fib: 3g | Sod: 150mg

LEMON AND YOGURT CAKE

Prep Time: 10 minutes
Cook Time: 20 minutes
Difficulty: 3/10
Category: Gluten-Free, Vegetarian

Ingredients:

- 100g plain flour (use gluten-free if necessary)
- 50g ground almonds
- 100g sugar
- 2 eggs
- 50ml olive oil
- Zest and juice of 1 lemon
- 50g Greek yogurt
- 1/2 tsp baking powder

Instructions:

1. Preheat the oven to 180°C (160°C fan). Grease a small cake tin.
2. In a bowl, whisk together the eggs and sugar until pale and fluffy.
3. Add the olive oil, lemon zest and juice, and yogurt, and mix well.
4. Sift in the flour, ground almonds, and baking powder, and fold gently into the mixture.
5. Pour the batter into the prepared cake tin and bake for 20 minutes, or until a skewer inserted into the center comes out clean.
6. Let cool before serving.

Nutritional Information:
Kcal: 300 | Carb: 36g | Pro: 6g | Fat: 14g | Fib: 2g | Sod: 100mg

104

PANNA COTTA WITH BERRY COMPOTE

Prep Time: 10 minutes (plus chilling time)
Cook Time: 5 minutes
Difficulty: 3/10
Category: Gluten-Free, Vegetarian

Ingredients:

- 200ml double cream
- 50g sugar
- 1 tsp vanilla extract
- 2 sheets gelatin (or 1 tsp gelatin powder)
- 100g mixed berries
- 1 tbsp honey

Instructions:

1. Soak the gelatin sheets in cold water until soft.
2. In a saucepan, heat the cream, sugar, and vanilla until the sugar dissolves. Do not boil.
3. Remove from heat and stir in the softened gelatin until dissolved.
4. Pour the mixture into ramekins and chill in the fridge for at least 4 hours.
5. For the compote, heat the berries and honey in a small saucepan until the berries soften and release their juices.
6. Let cool, then spoon over the panna cotta before serving.

Nutritional Information:
Kcal: 300 | Carb: 25g | Pro: 4g | Fat: 22g | Fib: 2g | Sod: 50mg

ROASTED PEARS WITH HONEY AND CINNAMON

Prep Time: 5 minutes
Cook Time: 10 minutes
Difficulty: 2/10
Category: Gluten-Free, Vegetarian

Ingredients:

- 2 ripe pears, halved and cored
- 2 tbsp honey
- 1/2 tsp ground cinnamon
- 1 tbsp butter

Instructions:

1. Preheat the oven to 200°C (180°C fan).
2. Place the pear halves in a baking dish, cut side up.
3. Drizzle with honey, sprinkle with cinnamon, and dot with butter.
4. Roast for 10 minutes, or until the pears are tender and golden.
5. Serve immediately.

Nutritional Information:
Kcal: 180 | Carb: 38g | Pro: 1g | Fat: 6g | Fib: 4g | Sod: 20mg

GREEK ALMOND COOKIES (AMYGDALOTA)

Prep Time: 10 minutes
Cook Time: 15 minutes
Difficulty: 3/10
Category: Gluten-Free, Vegetarian

Ingredients:

- 100g ground almonds
- 50g sugar
- 1 egg white
- 1/2 tsp almond extract
- Icing sugar, for dusting

Instructions:

1. Preheat the oven to 180°C (160°C fan). Line a baking tray with parchment paper.
2. In a bowl, mix the ground almonds, sugar, egg white, and almond extract until a dough forms.
3. Roll the dough into small balls and place them on the prepared baking tray.
4. Flatten slightly and dust with icing sugar.
5. Bake for 15 minutes, or until the edges are golden.
6. Let cool before serving.

Nutritional Information:
Kcal: 150 | Carb: 12g | Pro: 4g | Fat: 10g | Fib: 2g | Sod: 20mg

LEMON DRIZZLE CAKE

Prep Time: 10 minutes
Cook Time: 20 minutes
Difficulty: 3/10
Category: Gluten-Free, Vegetarian

Ingredients:

- 100g plain flour (use gluten-free if necessary)
- 100g sugar
- 2 eggs
- 50ml olive oil
- Zest and juice of 1 lemon
- 1/2 tsp baking powder
- 50g icing sugar

Instructions:

1. Preheat the oven to 180°C (160°C fan). Grease a small loaf tin.
2. In a bowl, whisk together the eggs and sugar until pale and fluffy.
3. Add the olive oil, lemon zest, and juice, and mix well.
4. Sift in the flour and baking powder, and fold gently into the mixture.
5. Pour the batter into the prepared loaf tin and bake for 20 minutes, or until a skewer inserted into the center comes out clean.
6. Mix the icing sugar with a little lemon juice to make a glaze, and drizzle over the cooled cake.

Nutritional Information:
Kcal: 300 | Carb: 50g | Pro: 6g | Fat: 10g | Fib: 2g | Sod: 100mg

CHOCOLATE AND OLIVE OIL MOUSSE

Prep Time: 10 minutes (plus chilling time)
Cook Time: 5 minutes
Difficulty: 3/10
Category: Gluten-Free, Vegetarian

Ingredients:

- 100g dark chocolate, chopped
- 2 tbsp olive oil
- 2 eggs, separated
- 50g sugar
- Pinch of salt

Instructions:

1. Melt the dark chocolate in a heatproof bowl over a pan of simmering water.
2. Stir in the olive oil and let cool slightly.
3. In a separate bowl, whisk the egg yolks and sugar until pale and thick.
4. Fold the chocolate mixture into the egg yolk mixture.
5. In another bowl, whisk the egg whites with a pinch of salt until stiff peaks form.
6. Fold the egg whites into the chocolate mixture until fully combined.
7. Spoon the mousse into serving glasses and chill in the fridge for at least 2 hours.
8. Serve chilled.

Nutritional Information:
Kcal: 300 | Carb: 28g | Pro: 5g | Fat: 20g | Fib: 4g | Sod: 40mg

SPICED ORANGE AND ALMOND MUFFINS

Prep Time: 10 minutes
Cook Time: 15 minutes
Difficulty: 3/10
Category: Gluten-Free, Vegetarian

Ingredients:

- 100g ground almonds
- 50g plain flour (use gluten-free if necessary)
- 100g sugar
- 2 eggs
- Zest and juice of 1 orange
- 50ml olive oil
- 1/2 tsp ground cinnamon
- 1/2 tsp baking powder

Instructions:

1. Preheat the oven to 180°C (160°C fan). Line a muffin tin with paper cases.
2. In a bowl, whisk together the eggs and sugar until pale and fluffy.
3. Add the olive oil, orange zest and juice, and ground cinnamon, and mix well.
4. Sift in the flour, ground almonds, and baking powder, and fold gently into the mixture.
5. Spoon the batter into the muffin cases and bake for 15 minutes, or until a skewer inserted into the center comes out clean.
6. Let cool before serving.

Nutritional Information:
Kcal: 200 | Carb: 28g | Pro: 4g | Fat: 10g | Fib: 2g | Sod: 80mg

HONEY AND SESAME SEED BARS (PASTELI)

Prep Time: 5 minutes
Cook Time: 10 minutes (plus cooling time)
Difficulty: 3/10
Category: Gluten-Free, Vegetarian

Ingredients:

- 100g sesame seeds
- 50g honey
- 1 tbsp olive oil

Instructions:

1. In a saucepan, heat the honey and olive oil over low heat until melted.
2. Stir in the sesame seeds and cook for 2-3 minutes until slightly toasted.
3. Pour the mixture onto a sheet of parchment paper and spread it out evenly.
4. Let cool completely, then cut into bars.
5. Serve immediately or store in an airtight container.

Nutritional Information:
Kcal: 200 | Carb: 20g | Pro: 4g | Fat: 12g | Fib: 4g | Sod: 20mg

MEDITERRANEAN FRUIT COMPOTE

Prep Time: 5 minutes
Cook Time: 10 minutes
Difficulty: 2/10
Category: Gluten-Free, Vegetarian, Vegan

Ingredients:

- 1 apple, peeled and diced
- 1 pear, peeled and diced
- 4 dried apricots, chopped
- 1 tbsp honey (optional)
- Juice of 1/2 lemon
- 1/2 tsp ground cinnamon

Instructions:

1. In a saucepan, combine the apple, pear, dried apricots, honey, lemon juice, and cinnamon.
2. Cook over medium heat for 10 minutes, or until the fruit is tender and the juices have thickened.
3. Serve warm or chilled.

Nutritional Information:
Kcal: 150 | Carb: 38g | Pro: 1g | Fat: 1g | Fib: 6g | Sod: 10mg

BAKED APPLES WITH CINNAMON AND NUTS

Prep Time: 5 minutes
Cook Time: 10 minutes
Difficulty: 2/10
Category: Gluten-Free, Vegetarian, Vegan

Ingredients:

- 2 apples, cored
- 2 tbsp chopped walnuts or almonds
- 2 tbsp raisins
- 1 tbsp honey
- 1/2 tsp ground cinnamon

Instructions:

1. Preheat the oven to 200°C (180°C fan).
2. Place the apples in a baking dish and fill the cores with chopped nuts and raisins.
3. Drizzle with honey and sprinkle with cinnamon.
4. Bake for 10 minutes, or until the apples are tender.
5. Serve immediately.

Nutritional Information:
Kcal: 200 | Carb: 40g | Pro: 2g | Fat: 6g | Fib: 6g | Sod: 10mg

Meal Plan

INTRODUCTION TO THE 30-DAY MEDITERRANEAN MEAL PLAN

Welcome to your 30-day Mediterranean meal plan, thoughtfully designed to provide you with a balanced, flavorful diet rich in the authentic tastes and health benefits of the Mediterranean. This plan has been carefully structured to incorporate a wide variety of nutritious dishes that align with the principles of the Mediterranean diet, renowned for its ability to promote optimal health and long-term well-being.

DIETARY CHOICES AND RATIONALE

Balance of Plant-Based and Animal-Based Foods: The foundation of this meal plan is rooted in a plant-based approach, with a significant emphasis on vegetables, legumes, whole grains, nuts, and seeds. These foods are packed with essential vitamins, minerals, and antioxidants, contributing to overall health and disease prevention. To maintain variety and ensure you receive a full spectrum of nutrients, we've included 2 meat-based and 2 fish-based meals each week. These provide high-quality protein, omega-3 fatty acids, and essential nutrients like iron and B vitamins.

Prioritizing Vegetarian and Vegan Options: Given the growing recognition of the benefits of plant-based diets, this plan prioritizes vegetarian and vegan meals. These dishes are not only rich in fiber and low in saturated fats but also help reduce environmental impact. The vegetarian and vegan meals are balanced to ensure they provide all the necessary macronutrients, particularly focusing on sources of plant-based protein like legumes, nuts, seeds, and whole grains.

INTEGRATING ADDITIONAL FOODS

Incorporating Bread and Other Staples: To complement the meals in this plan, consider

incorporating traditional Mediterranean staples such as whole-grain bread, pita, or wholemeal rolls. Bread can be an excellent source of additional fiber and energy, particularly when consumed in moderation and paired with healthy fats like olive oil. When choosing bread, opt for whole grain or wholemeal varieties to maximize nutrient intake.

Supplementing with Fresh Fruits and Dairy: Fresh fruit is a perfect addition to your meals or as a snack between them. Consider seasonal fruits like berries, apples, oranges, or pears. For those who consume dairy, adding a small serving of yogurt or a piece of cheese, such as feta or Parmesan, can enhance both the flavor and nutritional value of your meals.

TIPS FOR SUBSTITUTIONS AND MAINTAINING BALANCE

Substituting Proteins: If you need to substitute proteins, ensure that you maintain the nutritional balance by choosing options that provide similar macronutrient profiles. For example, if you replace a fish-based meal with a vegetarian option, consider using ingredients like chickpeas, lentils, or tofu to ensure adequate protein intake.

Adjusting to Dietary Preferences: This meal plan is versatile and can be adjusted to fit your dietary preferences or restrictions. If you prefer more plant-based days, simply substitute meat or fish dishes with vegetarian or vegan options from this plan. Conversely, if you require more protein from animal sources, you can replace some vegetarian meals with additional fish or lean meats.

Maintaining Portion Control: While the Mediterranean diet encourages the enjoyment of food, it's also important to practice mindful eating and portion control. This plan is designed to help you feel satisfied without overeating. When adding supplementary foods like bread or dairy, be mindful of portions to keep the meal balanced and in line with your dietary goals.

Final Thoughts

This 30-day Mediterranean meal plan is not just a guide but a journey towards healthier eating habits. By following this plan, you're embracing a lifestyle that celebrates whole foods, balanced nutrition, and the joy of eating well. Feel free to personalize it to suit your tastes and needs, and enjoy the process of discovering new flavors and dishes that nourish both your body and soul.

Remember, the key to the Mediterranean diet is balance, variety, and enjoying the experience of cooking and eating. Bon appétit!

DAY	BREAKFAST	LUNCH	DINNER
1	GREEK YOGURT WITH HONEY AND WALNUTS	GRILLED CHICKEN SOUVLAKI WITH TZATZIKI	BAKED COD WITH TOMATOES AND OLIVES
2	MEDITERRANEAN SCRAMBLED EGGS WITH SPINACH AND FETA	LENTIL AND BEETROOT SALAD WITH FETA	PAN-SEARED SEA BASS WITH CAPER SAUCE
3	AVOCADO TOAST WITH CHERRY TOMATOES AND OLIVE OIL	CHICKPEA AND SPINACH SOUP	ROASTED MEDITERRANEAN VEGETABLES WITH THYME
4	OVERNIGHT OATS WITH ALMONDS AND BERRIES	GREEK SALAD WITH FETA AND OLIVES	STUFFED PEPPERS WITH QUINOA AND FETA
5	TOMATO AND CUCUMBER BREAKFAST SALAD	MEDITERRANEAN QUINOA SALAD WITH CUCUMBER AND MINT	SLOW-COOKED LAMB SHOULDER WITH ROSEMARY
6	WHOLE GRAIN PORRIDGE WITH FRESH FRUITS AND NUTS	WARM FARRO AND ROASTED VEGETABLE SALAD	MEDITERRANEAN FISH STEW WITH SAFFRON
7	OLIVE OIL AND ORANGE CAKE MUFFINS	GRILLED VEGETABLE SALAD WITH BALSAMIC GLAZE	BAKED TROUT WITH ALMONDS AND HERBS
8	MEDITERRANEAN BREAKFAST WRAP WITH EGGS, SPINACH, AND FETA	STUFFED CHICKEN BREAST WITH SPINACH AND FETA	GRILLED CALAMARI WITH LEMON AND GARLIC
9	SAVORY GREEK YOGURT BOWL WITH OLIVES AND CUCUMBERS	TUSCAN WHITE BEAN AND KALE SOUP	BAKED SALMON WITH A MUSTARD-DILL GLAZE
10	RICOTTA AND HONEY ON WHOLE GRAIN TOAST	LENTIL AND BEETROOT SALAD WITH FETA	ROASTED CAULIFLOWER WITH CUMIN AND CORIANDER
11	HERBED FRITTATA WITH COURGETTES AND PARMESAN	LAMB KOFTA WITH MINT YOGURT	RATATOUILLE WITH FRESH HERBS
12	CHIA PUDDING WITH ALMOND MILK AND FRESH FRUIT	CAPRESE SALAD WITH FRESH BASIL AND BALSAMIC REDUCTION	MUSSELS IN WHITE WINE AND GARLIC
13	SPINACH AND MUSHROOM BREAKFAST QUESADILLA	GREEK CHICKPEA SALAD WITH LEMON VINAIGRETTE	ROASTED BUTTERNUT SQUASH WITH SAGE
14	LEMON AND POPPY SEED BREAKFAST LOAF	TABBOULEH WITH FRESH PARSLEY AND MINT	GRILLED ASPARAGUS WITH LEMON AND OLIVE OIL
15	FIG AND WALNUT BREAKFAST BARS	GRILLED CHICKEN SOUVLAKI WITH TZATZIKI	BAKED COD WITH TOMATOES AND OLIVES

DAY	BREAKFAST	LUNCH	DINNER
16	GRILLED HALLOUMI AND TOMATO SANDWICH	MEDITERRANEAN QUINOA SALAD WITH CUCUMBER AND MINT	PAN-SEARED SEA BASS WITH CAPER SAUCE
17	MEDITERRANEAN BREAKFAST BOWL WITH QUINOA AND HUMMUS	WARM FARRO AND ROASTED VEGETABLE SALAD	SPAGHETTI WITH CLAMS (SPAGHETTI ALLE VONGOLE)
18	SMOKED SALMON AND AVOCADO ON RYE BREAD	GREEK SALAD WITH FETA AND OLIVES	BRAISED GREEN BEANS WITH TOMATOES AND ONIONS
19	EGG AND VEGETABLE BREAKFAST MUFFINS	SLOW-COOKED LAMB SHOULDER WITH ROSEMARY	GRILLED SARDINES WITH LEMON AND HERBS
20	RICOTTA PANCAKES WITH BERRIES	MEDITERRANEAN QUINOA SALAD WITH CUCUMBER AND MINT	BAKED SALMON WITH A MUSTARD-DILL GLAZE
21	GREEK YOGURT WITH HONEY AND WALNUTS	GREEK CHICKPEA SALAD WITH LEMON VINAIGRETTE	BAKED TOMATOES STUFFED WITH RICE AND HERBS
22	MEDITERRANEAN SCRAMBLED EGGS WITH SPINACH AND FETA	GRILLED VEGETABLE SALAD WITH BALSAMIC GLAZE	GRILLED TUNA STEAK WITH FRESH HERBS
23	AVOCADO TOAST WITH CHERRY TOMATOES AND OLIVE OIL	TABBOULEH WITH FRESH PARSLEY AND MINT	STUFFED PEPPERS WITH QUINOA AND FETA
24	OVERNIGHT OATS WITH ALMONDS AND BERRIES	MEDITERRANEAN ORZO SALAD WITH SUN-DRIED TOMATOES	SPAGHETTI WITH CLAMS (SPAGHETTI ALLE VONGOLE)
25	TOMATO AND CUCUMBER BREAKFAST SALAD	PORK TENDERLOIN WITH GARLIC AND THYME	GRILLED TUNA STEAK WITH FRESH HERBS
26	WHOLE GRAIN PORRIDGE WITH FRESH FRUITS AND NUTS	MEDITERRANEAN ORZO SALAD WITH SUN-DRIED TOMATOES	VEGETARIAN RATATOUILLE
27	OLIVE OIL AND ORANGE CAKE MUFFINS	CAPRESE SALAD WITH FRESH BASIL AND BALSAMIC REDUCTION	BALSAMIC GLAZED BRUSSELS SPROUTS
28	MEDITERRANEAN BREAKFAST WRAP WITH EGGS, SPINACH, AND FETA	GRILLED CHICKEN SOUVLAKI WITH TZATZIKI	BAKED COD WITH TOMATOES AND OLIVES
29	SAVORY GREEK YOGURT BOWL WITH OLIVES AND CUCUMBERS	GREEK SALAD WITH FETA AND OLIVES	STUFFED PEPPERS WITH QUINOA AND FETA
30	RICOTTA AND HONEY ON WHOLE GRAIN TOAST	LAMB KOFTA WITH MINT YOGURT	MEDITERRANEAN BAKED FISH WITH VEGETABLES

Shopping List

ESSENTIAL PANTRY AND INGREDIENT LIST FOR THE MEDITERRANEAN DIET

To help you prepare for the 30-day Mediterranean meal plan, here's a comprehensive shopping list divided into two sections: essential pantry staples and weekly shopping lists. The pantry staples are items that you should always have on hand, while the weekly lists are tailored to the recipes you'll be making each week.

ESSENTIAL PANTRY STAPLES

These are the foundational ingredients that are commonly used throughout the meal plan. Keep these stocked in your kitchen to ensure you're always ready to cook Mediterranean-inspired meals.

- Olive Oil (Extra Virgin)
- Balsamic Vinegar
- Red Wine Vinegar
- Lemon Juice
- Garlic (fresh and powder)
- Onions (yellow, red)
- Dried Herbs (oregano, thyme, rosemary, basil)
- Spices (ground cumin, ground coriander, cinnamon, smoked paprika)
- Salt (sea salt or kosher salt)
- Pepper (black pepper)
- Honey
- Whole-Grain Bread or Pita
- Whole-Grain Pasta
- Brown Rice or Quinoa
- Canned Tomatoes (diced, crushed)
- Canned Chickpeas (and other beans)
- Nuts and Seeds (almonds, walnuts, pine nuts, sesame seeds)
- Tahini
- Greek Yogurt
- Feta Cheese
- Parmesan Cheese
- Dijon Mustard
- Capers
- Sun-Dried Tomatoes
- Olives (Kalamata or other varieties)
- Anchovy Fillets
- Frozen Vegetables (peas, spinach)

WEEKLY SHOPPING LISTS

WEEK 1:

FRUITS & VEGETABLES:

- 4 Tomatoes
- 2 Cucumbers
- 1 Bunch Spinach
- 2 Red Peppers
- 1 Lemon
- 1 Courgette (Zucchini)
- 1 Aubergine (Eggplant)
- 1 Bunch Fresh Parsley
- 1 Bunch Fresh Mint
- 1 Bunch Fresh Basil
- 1 Bunch Asparagus
- 1 Head Cauliflower

PROTEINS & DAIRY:

- 4 Chicken Breasts
- 2 Cod Fillets
- 1 Pack Feta Cheese
- 1 Pack Halloumi Cheese

GRAINS & BREAD:

- Whole Grain Bread
- Brown Rice
- Quinoa

WEEK 2:

FRUITS & VEGETABLES:

- 2 Avocados
- 2 Lemons
- 1 Bunch Spinach
- 2 Red Peppers
- 2 Courgettes (Zucchini)
- 1 Aubergine (Eggplant)
- 1 Bunch Fresh Parsley
- 1 Bunch Fresh Mint
- 1 Bunch Fresh Basil
- 1 Bunch Thyme
- 1 Head Broccoli

PROTEINS & DAIRY:

- 2 Salmon Fillets
- 2 Chicken Breasts
- 1 Pack Greek Yogurt
- 1 Pack Ricotta Cheese
- 1 Pack Parmesan Cheese

GRAINS & BREAD:

- Whole Grain Pasta
- Quinoa

WEEK 3:

FRUITS & VEGETABLES:

- 2 Lemons
- 1 Bunch Spinach
- 1 Bunch Fresh Parsley
- 2 Courgettes (Zucchini)
- 1 Aubergine (Eggplant)
- 1 Bunch Fresh Mint
- 1 Bunch Fresh Basil
- 1 Head Broccoli
- 1 Head Cauliflower
- 4 Tomatoes

PROTEINS & DAIRY:

- 2 Trout Fillets
- 2 Lamb Chops
- 1 Pack Feta Cheese
- 1 Pack Greek Yogurt

GRAINS & BREAD:

- Whole Grain Bread
- Brown Rice
- Quinoa

WEEK 4:

FRUITS & VEGETABLES:

- 2 Avocados
- 2 Lemons
- 1 Bunch Spinach
- 2 Red Peppers
- 2 Courgettes (Zucchini)
- 1 Bunch Fresh Parsley
- 1 Bunch Fresh Mint
- 1 Bunch Fresh Basil
- 1 Bunch Thyme
- 1 Head Broccoli
- 1 Head Cauliflower

PROTEINS & DAIRY:

- 2 Chicken Breasts
- 2 Salmon Fillets
- 1 Pack Greek Yogurt
- 1 Pack Feta Cheese

GRAINS & BREAD:

- Whole Grain Bread
- Brown Rice
- Whole Grain Pasta

TIPS FOR GROCERY SHOPPING AND SUBSTITUTIONS

- **Buying Fresh Produce:** Try to buy fruits and vegetables in season for the best flavor and nutritional value. Organic options are preferable when available.
- **Storing Essentials:** Keep nuts, seeds, and grains in airtight containers to preserve freshness. Olive oil should be stored in a cool, dark place.
- **Substitutions:** If you need to substitute an ingredient, try to keep the nutritional profile similar. For example, if you're out of quinoa, brown rice or barley can be good alternatives.
- **Batch Cooking:** Consider cooking grains and legumes in larger batches at the beginning of the week and storing them in the fridge. This can save time and help you quickly assemble meals.

This shopping list and the meal plan are designed to make your Mediterranean diet journey both enjoyable and practical. By having the right ingredients on hand, you can ensure your meals are nutritious, delicious, and easy to prepare.

Copyright 2024-2025 by Maggie Mabel - All rights reserved.

This document aims to provide accurate and reliable information on the subject and issues addressed.

The publication is sold with the understanding that the publisher is not obligated to provide accounting services, officially authorized services, or other qualified services. If legal or professional advice is needed, it should be sought from a professional in the relevant field.

Excerpt from a statement of principles accepted and equally approved by a committee of the American Bar Association and a committee of publishers and associations. It is illegal to reproduce, duplicate, or transmit any part of this document, whether electronically or in printed form. Recording this publication is strictly prohibited, and any storage of this document is not allowed, except with written permission from the publisher. All rights reserved.

The information provided in this document is intended to be truthful and consistent, and any liability, whether due to negligence or otherwise, arising from the use or misuse of the policies, processes, or instructions contained herein, rests solely with the recipient reader.

Under no circumstances shall the publisher be liable for any compensation, damages, or monetary loss resulting from the use of this site, damages, or financial losses due to the information contained in this document, whether directly or indirectly.

The respective authors and publishers hold all copyrights. The information contained in this document is provided for informational purposes only and is universal as such.

The presentation of the information is without contract or warranty of any kind. Trademarks used are without consent, and the publication of the trademark is without the permission or endorsement of the trademark owner.

All trademarks and registered trademarks mentioned in this book are for clarification purposes only and belong to their respective owners, who are not affiliated with this document.

Printed in Dunstable, United Kingdom